The Life and Crimes of Errol Flynn

The Life and Crimes of Errol Flynn

LIONEL GODFREY

With illustrations from the Rick Dodd Collection

ST MARTIN'S PRESS
NEW YORK

For information, write:
St. Martin's Press, Inc., 175 Fifth Ave., New York,
N.Y. 10010.
Manufactured in the United States of America
Library of Congress Catalog Card Number: 77-72302

Library of Congress Cataloging in Publication Data

Godfrey, Lionel.
The life and crimes of Errol Flynn.

Bibliography: p. 159
Discography: p. 166
Filmography: p. 161
Includes index.
1. Flynn, Errol Leslie, 1909-1959. 2. Moving-picture actors and actresses—United States—Biography. I. Title
PN2287.F55G6 1977 791.43'028'0924 [B] 77-72302
ISBN 0-312-48385-6

Contents

Illustrations

Between pages 32 and 33

Between pages 80 and 81

PICTURE CREDITS

Warner Brothers: 2, 5-11,14,15,18-20,26,28; Keystone Press Agency: 12; *Movie Life*: 16; Sport and General: 4; United Press International: 25; *Daily Express*: 27; Universal: 30; Regal Films: 32; 20th Century Fox: 33, 34.

At some time or other, haven't you tried to tell your children about the great moment in *The Adventures of Robin Hood* when Errol Flynn strode into the castle with a deer on his shoulders, or about the way Alan Hale, as Little John, roared with laughter?

Pauline Kael
Kiss Kiss Bang Bang

In tragic life, God wot,
No villain need be! Passions spin the plot:
We are betrayed by what is false within.

Meredith

For

RICK

custodian of the memories

and for

MAUREEN

who lived through the great adventure

The Life and Crimes of Errol Flynn

Foreword

Errol Flynn was a great star in an age of great stars. James Cagney had a more aggressive virility; Humphrey Bogart and Clark Gable offered indigenous, contemporary masculinity; James Stewart was recognizably the product of rural America and traditional values; Cary Grant was the polished, witty lover; and Tyrone Power displayed heart-fluttering, dark good-looks. But Flynn, aided by his most famous films, had a timeless, universal appeal, and though he was fond of claiming that he had been born into the wrong century, he could have fitted into any era. His stunning handsomeness belonged to no particular age or decade. In the type of role for which he is best remembered, he had no rival. Manners of his kind, though they may be temporarily scorned and laughed at, can never really go out of style: his punctiliousness was directed towards men as well as women.

I am an unashamed Flynn apologist. When I was growing up, he was my idol, and though such enthusiasms are often repudiated by their possessors or at least modified in their allegedly mature years, mine has altered only to grow in intensity. It is not the adulation of a fan, since I am critical of his limitations as an actor and aware of his tragic defects as a man. But his influence upon me has been incalculable. To take just one example, my manners, whether good or bad, are modelled on his own.

Nor am I alone in my admiration. Thousands have felt and continue to feel the fascination of Errol Flynn.

Such a man is very rare, not to say unique. He had, this book ventures to suggest, qualities both as a filmstar and a person that have been combined in no other. He was the greatest charmer in the world, even to those who had cause to hate him, even to those who had never met him in person.

Perhaps, one might add sadly, *especially* to those who had never met him in person.

Out of my enthusiasm comes this biography – an attempt to delineate and explain a man and an actor, a legend and a joke, an author *manqué* and a real enigma. If the picture is not consistent, then neither was the subject. But if the colours are not vivid and arresting, then Errol Flynn cannot be blamed.

However, part of my intention has been to correct an imbalance in other views of my subject. The Flynn films have been ably discussed in articles and books, and there is a comparatively recent volume that painstakingly examines the fact and fiction of his pre-Hollywood years. Virtually the remainder of a vast outpouring of printed words – not excluding Flynn's autobiography, *My Wicked, Wicked Ways* – has tended to concentrate on the lurid and sensational aspects of his life. Although I have made no attempt to deny these or to gloss over them, I have aimed to place them in the context of a career that had its quieter side and facets more complicated, not to say more rewarding, than a notorious rape-trial. Unfortunately, both during his lifetime and since, journalists have been inspired by the crimes of Errol Flynn to the near-exclusion of the man's other activities and qualities. If the reader concludes that the word "crimes" in the title of this biography is ironic, the author will not object.

My deep gratitude must be expressed to my wife, who did most of the research needed to supplement a lifelong interest. Very special thanks are also due to Rick Dodd, both for his encouragement and for helping me select illustrations from his unique collection of Flynn memorabilia and photographs. A few years ago, a television show led me to the fascinating discovery that Rick lived almost literally on my doorstep and possessed a veritable treasure-trove bearing testimony to years of devotion to his subject. Neither he nor my wife can be held responsible for any shortcomings of the book that follows.

I must acknowledge my debt to the stimulus and information provided by: *The Films of Errol Flynn* by Tony Thomas, Rudy Behlmer and Clifford McCarty (Citadel Press, New York,

1969), *Errol and Me* by Nora Eddington (Signet Books, New York, 1960), and *Bring On The Empty Horses* by David Niven (Hamish Hamilton Limited, London, 1975).

I should like to thank those concerned for permission to quote from: *My Wicked, Wicked Ways* by Errol Flynn (G. P. Putnam's Sons, New York, 1959; Laurence Pollinger Limited, London); *The Young Errol* by John Hammond Moore (Angus and Robertson, Sydney, 1975); *Adventure in Repertory* by Aubrey Dyas (Jarrold and Sons Limited, London, 1948); *The Celluloid Muse* by Charles Higham and Joel Greenberg (Angus and Robertson Limited, London, 1969); and *Huston at Fontainebleau* by Cynthia Grenier (The British Film Institute, London, as publishers of *Sight and Sound,* Autumn, 1958).

I should like also to express my gratitude to Sterling Hayden for permission to quote from his *Wanderer* (first published by Alfred A. Knopf Incorporated, New York, 1963).

I have reprinted in this book several passages from *Beam Ends* by Errol Flynn (Cassell and Company Limited, London, 1937). As a result of the destruction of archives during World War II, it has been impossible to establish ownership of the copyright of this work.

LIONEL GODFREY

Introduction

Vernon (Lefty) Gomez once said, "I'd rather be lucky than good", a stimulating reflection coming from a baseball-star, or anyone else for that matter. Errol Flynn was certainly lucky. He might also be said – dependent on one's interpretation of the word – to have been good.

Errol Leslie Thomson Flynn died on 14th October 1959. He just made it to fifty, but if that half-century was a near thing, there was no such sense of strain about his becoming a legend: Errol achieved it in his short lifetime – and with at least fifteen years to spare.

The legend, however, is a distorting glass through which to view both the actor and the man, and it is founded on a mish-mash of truth, gossip and invention as much as on the scenarios of his films. On the screen, one is repeatedly told, Flynn merely played himself, and yet pictures of Errol the man painted by others and in his autobiography often provide eloquent testimony to the falsity of the idea. Nor is it true that in most of his roles, even those for which he is best remembered, he was *only* a swashbuckler and a freebooter, a laughing daredevil in the style of Douglas Fairbanks. The actor of fact and the actor depicted by popular journalism ("just happened to look well in doublet and hose") did not correspond more than superficially, and in a deeper way the disparity between his movie-roles and his personal life was a real and a fascinating one.

Offscreen and onscreen, he was supposed to be a hellraiser, but both parts of the legend are grotesquely oversimplified. All the romantic heroes Flynn played – typically, sea-captains, adventurers, Don Juan, the bandit of Sherwood Forest, cavalry officers and gallant gentlemen – were uncomplicated characters, unwaveringly on the side of a right that, unlike

Errol, they would not have dreamed of questioning. They were more often grave than lighthearted, frequently leading others less serious back to duty, and the true hellraiser in many Flynn pictures was the great Alan Hale, to whom Errol behaved on screen, despite chronology, like an older brother – tolerant of his flippancy but also custodian of his morality.

As for the man, he, too, differed greatly from the Errol Flynn who was the delight and to some extent the invention of columnists during his Hollywood years. The first half of his life was colourful, exotic, shameful and shameless, and largely fiction, most of it fashioned by Flynn himself, for the man was a near-pathological liar or, if that judgement is too harsh, a great teller of tall tales. Later, in Hollywood, he appeared to romp through brawls, bars and boudoirs. Indeed, he *was* a hellraiser. He liked the company of men, particularly his friends Alan Hale, Bruce Cabot and Guinn 'Big Boy' Williams, all of whom worked in his pictures, and he enjoyed drinking and practical jokes. He once concealed a dead snake in Olivia de Havilland's panties. In many ways, he was careless and irresponsible. To some, immune to his charm, his company was insufferable. He loved honesty, deflated hypocrisy and once said, "I never worry about money so long as I can reconcile my net income with my gross habits." He certainly lived lavishly, enjoying himself immensely, and throughout his life he was not too punctilious about settling debts. Two rape-accusations brought against him failed laughably and, to the unreflective, confirmed his reputation as a modern Casanova. He could be a poseur. David Niven last saw him in 1958, when Flynn appeared to be at peace with himself and said he had discovered the Bible. It is hard to view the picture without some scepticism, an intuition that he might have been striking one more pose.

Nobody could deny these many facets to his character, and it is instructive to contrast them with the Errol beheld on the screen by many who, like me, were growing up in the 'forties and saw in him the perfect romantic hero. For, ironically, the screen Errol was a lover more spiritual than sexy. His love-scenes are among the most chastely poetic ever shot. In any case, the man found making love in front of the camera inhibiting and at rehearsals would simply say "Clinch" or "Embrace" at the appropriate moment. In his pictures, he is almost excessively gallant towards leading ladies like Brenda Marshall *(The Sea Hawk),* Alexis Smith *(San Antonio)* and Olivia de Havilland, who was teamed with him in a whole string of films. The screen Errol was always the considerate, courteous lover, true flower of chivalry – devoid of any whiff of carnality. Even *The Adventures of Don Juan* presents a Don at least as noble as he is philandering, as much concerned with epigrams as with underskirts and apparently quite ready to settle down with the 'right' woman – a Don strongly dissimilar to, say, Mozart's Don Giovanni, who is prepared to descend unregenerate into the flames and is much closer to Flynn the man.

There was far more to Errol Flynn than either his celluloid personality or his popular reputation. The hellraiser had his serious – even sinister – side. Whatever mistakes he made, he was in the best sense a hedonist. ("I wish they would not call me a 'hedonist'," Walter Pater once said. "It produces such a bad effect on people who don't know Greek.") Errol saw it as his moral duty to pursue happiness and fulfil his destiny. His quest took him along some doubtful routes. At a time before it became fashionable, he experimented with drugs – to ill effect. There was an ambivalence in his attitude towards women, whom he both enjoyed and used, loved and hated. He certainly saw them as predators, and if he had been asked what he hated most about them, he might well have answered, as the late Paul Douglas did, "Alimony". His bitterness towards divorce-lawyers and his first wife, Lili Damita, was enduring. He found marriage an impossible institution and said so repeatedly. He outraged moralists, whom he hated as much as the idea of putting his life into cold-storage.

These facets were noted, perhaps, but in general they were poorly understood. For example, his love of the sea was lifelong and genuine, though he probably knew less of ships than he pretended. The pretence, however, was enough to impress most people. There was a parallel in his undoubted urge to write. He published three books, none of them satisfactory, all of them revealing a real but deeply flawed – not to say limited – talent. As he grew older, his drinking, once lighthearted at least, became obsessive and sinister, but to most he was just an actor 'who drank'.

There was a gentle, reserved side to Errol's nature that baffled some and totally eluded others. He was neither unintelligent nor insensitive, and as the years went by, he became steadily disillusioned with Hollywood and found unbearably irksome the screen-roles allotted to him. As Louise Brooks has pointed out, stars like Flynn, striking for more pay and better parts, were fair game for the studios, who had all the power, saved money while the actors' salaries were suspended and obtained a good deal of free and helpful publicity for as long as their players tried to buck the system. As on the screen, Errol's guns, it seemed, were loaded with blanks. To cap it all, he soon ostensibly considered himself a ham, a strictly limited actor who had taken to 'walking through' his parts. To his critics, however, he was just another spoiled star, an ingrate who was biting the hand that fed him.

It is easy, then, to see why the legend persists. The legend is simple. The man was not.

1

The Perfect Specimen

He was born on 20th June 1909, in Hobart, Tasmania. His father was Professor Theodore Thomson Flynn, a marine biologist of distinction. At the time of Errol's birth, Theodore Flynn was a lecturer at the University of Tasmania, and two years later, he became Ralston Professor of Biology. Errol's mother was Lily Mary Young but she later changed her name to Marelle – perhaps, it has been suggested, to keep her identity clear after her son had married Lili Damita. On his mother's side, Errol was descended from a mariner who sailed on the *Bounty* and was with Fletcher Christian on Pitcairn Island.

Good looks are incalculable and unpredictable, and photographs of the Flynn parents, though their faces show character, sound structure and fine eyes, do not, even with hindsight, suggest the features of a son whose beauty was to be sighed over by women in all parts of the world. Both father and mother were Australians – a point worth stressing because of the name and because of the later fiction publicized by Warner Brothers of Errol's Irish background, an invention he himself worked hard and unceasingly to reinforce.

If Errol resembled either parent in temperament or appearance, it was his mother, but their relationship, as he described it in his autobiography, was tempestuous. In *Cads and Cavaliers,* Tony Thomas states that Errol suspected that his mother had been unfaithful to his father. If Errol's harbouring of this suspicion is accepted as true, his maturer years shape up even more promisingly as a happy hunting-ground for analysts. "From about four or five," he wrote, "I began one long unending scrap with my mother." After Errol's death, she was to join with his father in suggesting that he had been a perfect son, but as late as 1946, Marelle told a

New York reporter that Errol had been a nasty little boy. Or as he put it when they were both alive, "As she tells it today, I was a devil in boy's clothing."

The "unending scrap" did not remain at the same pitch, either, but got worse. Probably Marelle Flynn had a shock, if only of recognition, when she read these words in the posthumously published *My Wicked, Wicked Ways:*

"Our war deepened so that a time came when it was a matter of indifference to me whether I saw her or not.

"These brawls with her, almost daily occurrences, did something to me.

"Mostly I wanted to get away from her, get away from home."

This utterance is doubly interesting. First, it helps to explain Errol's *Wanderlust* that remained with him all his life. Second, and more importantly, it sheds light on his later attitude to women, since almost any woman he cared for was always the enemy as well as the desired one. In his only novel, *Showdown,* Errol described how his hero struggled with "his secret sense of guilt for never having loved [his mother]". The passage, like much of what he wrote in his books and articles, has a strongly autobiographical flavour.

With his father, on the other hand, the relationship was almost ideal – certainly as Errol looked back on it years later: "The rapport was with my father." He loved to join Professor Flynn on scientific jaunts and admired him almost to the point of idolatry. His father asserted after Flynn's death that his son could have been a good scientist. In an interview with Alan Trengrove of *The Sun,* Professor Flynn related that Errol, even at the age of five or six, would take in his father's conversation with other scientists, and he one day startled Theodore by scooping out of the water what he called, quite correctly, *pycnogonida* ('thick knees') – the class of sea-spiders that have enormous legs. Not only had the boy Errol remembered the word, he also pronounced it flawlessly.

Errol had a sister, Rosemary, who was two or three years his junior. He is significantly vague about the age-gap in *My Wicked, Wicked Ways,* and it seems probable that, in a two-child family of that kind, he did not see much of her when he was growing up. He has so little to say about her in his autobiography that it might also be supposed, even allowing for the age- and sex-differential, that the Flynn family was not closely knit. It was certainly not ideal. But, then, few families are.

Aside from the developing strife with his mother, Errol's pre-school years appear to have been normal and uneventful, though he adorned them in *My Wicked, Wicked Ways* with the usual episodes that make an uncritical reading of that book like tiptoeing through a minefield. One characteristically outrageous story concerns the young Errol, some ducks, a quantity of pork and a long piece of string. The net result as he reported it was that "in a few minutes [he] had a half-dozen ducks tied together beak to rectum on this greased string". (Exactly how the feat was allegedly performed, readers with strong stomachs can find out for themselves from the autobiography.)

Errol's first school was Franklin House School in Hobart, but by 1918 he was enrolled at a very good private school, Hutchins, his stay at which was to be followed in April 1920 by a year at the Friends School in North Hobart as the Flynns moved and lived at various addresses. Though he had not yet landed in serious trouble, a pattern of recalcitrance was already emerging in Errol. His arrogance and boredom with academic disciplines were observable.

At an uncertain date in the early 'twenties, Errol and his father left for London, whence they returned in June 1924. No clear picture of what Errol was doing during the interim has been found except in his autobiography, the truthfulness of which becomes highly suspect at this point. According to *My Wicked, Wicked Ways,* he went to a junior school called South-West London College, midway between Putney and Hammersmith and with an assistant headmaster named Sir Worthbottom Smith *(sic),* a down-at-heel aristocrat. "There opened," Errol wrote later, "two of the most dismal years of my life." All this might be easier to swallow if any record of the existence of South-West London College had been found. Fictitious or not, the school had a standard of scholarship that was "ridiculous". More interesting, however, than the 'facts' is a view that Errol articulated more than thirty years later – "after I was dropped into this school I was pretty much neglected by my parents".

In 1924, he was back in Tasmania, where on 14th July he enrolled in Hobart High School. At that time he was living with his father in a boarding house, Marelle being still in Europe, whither she had followed her husband and son, perhaps in 1922. Professor and Mrs Flynn frequently spent long periods apart – a loose arrangement that might have coloured the grown-up Errol's attitude to marriage. Marelle, evidence suggests, was an attractive woman who knew how to enjoy herself, and Theodore was rumoured to have had at least one romantic entanglement at about this time.

For the boyish pranks that were eventually to modulate into the insensitive practical jokes that were so much a part of the man, Errol was "asked to leave" Hobart High in 1925. At his various schools, the intuitive rebel was making his mark in sports, particularly boxing and swimming, but the bread-and-butter business of lessons was proving hard for his wayward nature to take. It was ever to be so.

The next stop was Sydney Church of England Grammar School, at which he lasted from March to August of 1926. Having been expelled, possibly for being caught *in flagrante delicto* on a coal-pile with the daughter of a laundress, he took his first job as a clerk with the shipping firm of Dalgety and Company in that year. His formal education had finished soon after his seventeenth birthday.

With knowledge of later history, it is clear even from this brief summary that Errol's life so far had already included characteristic, recurring themes of his career as a man – scandalous behaviour, travel, athletic pre-eminence and, by no means least, an aura of sexual adventure.

At this point, a discourse on authenticity may well be helpful.

"The exaggeration that is false," wrote the playwright Benn Levy, "is told by the politician. The exaggeration that is true is told by the artist." One might add that the exaggeration that is somewhere in a no-man's-land between fact and fantasy is the one so typically told by Errol Flynn.

In 1958 when he came to write *My Wicked, Wicked Ways,* though he was aided in his task, he imposed on the autobiography the quirks of a man who for thirty years had rarely hesitated to embroider, fabricate, colour or touch up the good tales that columnists and journalists seized upon so eagerly as copy.

Like the story – pure fiction – that he had boxed for Australia in the 1928 Olympics. (In the previous year, Errol *had* been a contender in the New South Wales state amateur boxing championships, from which he was eliminated by a bigger and stronger opponent. The Olympics story probably originated with the Warner Brothers publicity-department rather than with Errol, for once.)

Or the tale of his service in the Hong Kong Volunteers in the 'thirties.

Errol always listed this stint in *Who's Who* entries, but there is no record of his service with the corps and none of his putative contemporaries could remember him – a filmstar whose name had been linked with two rape-charges and all those lovely young ladies.

Throughout his adult life, Errol's attitude seemed to be: why spoil a good yarn with a crippling regard for the facts?

But he was not a complete liar. On the contrary, one is sometimes taken aback by the hard grain of truth embedded in an otherwise spurious account, and his tall tales do tend to be just those – exaggeration more frequently than total fabrication. Nevertheless, the tendency was pronounced, and the first part of the autobiography, *Tasmanian Devil, 1909–1927,* is full not only of questionable statements but also of wrong names and dates, improbable geography and inadequate chronology.

In *The Young Errol,* John Hammond Moore has undertaken so completely the examination of error and exposure of fiction in this section of *My Wicked, Wicked Ways* that I do not propose to labour the point in these pages that Errol's account is highly suspect. In any case, even without Dr Moore's brilliant demolition-work, perceptive readers of the autobiography will spot the more outrageous Flynn stories – those in which the truth-factor sinks to five per cent or even lower.

My own favourite comes slightly later in *My Wicked, Wicked Ways* and concerns a fight with a rickshaw-man in Pondicherry. When he literally pushed Errol for a tip, our young hero threw a punch at the man's chin – or where he thought it would be. But he failed to connect, and the other produced a knife gleaming "like quicksilver" – "and in a single fast stroke he cut my guts from my scrotum to the navel". Yelling at Errol to stand up straight, his friend Koets grabbed hold of the Flynn intestines and stuffed them back inside before he held Errol's belly closed with one hand.

What presence of mind. What a story.

There are more in similar vein. In fact, the reader comes to expect their regular appearance, since Errol composed *My Wicked, Wicked Ways* loosely to a formula: every few pages, a thrilling exploit or an amorous adventure. Of course, later in the book, dealing with matters easier to verify, he was more accurate. But there are still interpolations of pure fiction, and there are still the lapses in chronology and blurring of important details.

To sum up, the further one goes back into Errol's life, the more unreliable is the information that he himself provided. In the pages that follow, I have endeavoured, with the map provided by John Hammond Moore, to stick fairly closely to the safe trail of fact and to skirt the treacherous quicksands of exaggeration, though I have sometimes erected a sign to point out which lies where.

In the 'thirties, when Errol was in the Olympiads, a conversation-club whose membership included John Barrymore, W. C. Fields and Gene Fowler, he would sometimes regale them with tales of his experiences in New Guinea. Formidable tellers of stories that they were themselves, "they lifted their eyebrows sceptically", Errol wrote.

Who could blame them?

The job with Dalgety and Company in Sydney was to last almost exactly a year.

During that time, Errol became friendly with the Dibbs family, whom he described as very "correct, serious". More accurately, they were probably conservative, part of the local commercial and political establishment, but Errol had good times with the younger generation and their friends. There were three daughters, to one of whom, Naomi, Errol was briefly engaged several years later. It may be guessed that the parents had some reservations about this young man, charming and amusing though he might be. He was a rebel and something of a show-off, if undoubtedly excellent at sports, and to such affluent people his prospects could not have looked too good.

Errol's prospects were to become even poorer. In 1927, soon after his elimination from the New South Wales amateur boxing championships, he was sacked from Dalgety and Company for theft. This was scarcely grand larceny, and a friend said that the money involved was later paid back; but it did reveal Errol's tendency to cut corners – a predilection shared by many other young men before and since, but one that was ineradicably part of the Flynn character, then as subsequently. Without references, he hung about Sydney for three weeks before making the first of his journeys to New Guinea.

Since Errol was at this time living with his grandmother, his own account of sleeping in a park at night with bums – "swagmen" or "sundowners" – is not to be trusted, any more than one can believe that after a fight with Naomi Dibbs he sold her engagement ring to raise his fare to New Guinea. Just to obfuscate matters still more, Errol wrote in his autobiography that he sailed in 1926.

The facts are that he arrived in Rabaul on 1st October, 1927, having sailed on the *Montoro* to what was the gateway to New Guinea. "From then on," he said later, "I began the wanderings that have never ceased."

2

In the Wake of the Bounty

But why New Guinea?

There could have been several other reasons, but in September the Sydney newspapers had been full of stories of the discovery of gold there, and to Errol, who was on the threshold of life and had already been in one scrape for lack of money, the possibilities of finding what others had discovered must have been enticing. But he was not to get to the goldfields for some time. Owing to his feckless ways, he spent the next twenty-five months in a variety of jobs, most of which he would suddenly quit if he did not first get fired. He was drinking, out on the town as often as he could be and congenitally lazy. Of his later employment as a government cadet, he wrote, "Naturally the work soon became a bore," and that word "naturally" is symptomatic of his attitude to wage-slavery or a modicum of responsibility.

Despite the ever-present threat of malaria, Errol found life in Rabaul as colourful and carefree as he had hoped it would be, and he was appointed as a government cadet, to be trained as a patrol officer. The nature of this appointment was temporary or provisional until his references in Sydney had been confirmed. There was some suggestion of 'influence' about Errol's entry, but it was also true that one of the six young men who had won these prized posts that year had dropped out.

Errol was assigned to Kokopo, where he soon found a niche for himself in the social life, his popularity having much to do with his fine tennis and swimming. But he was not to stay there for long. After a few weeks, the *Montoro* returned to Rabaul, bringing with it letters from Dalgety and Company. What they said – or did not say, damningly – can be imagined by the fact that Errol's dismissal from government service followed immediately. His career as a cadet had been spectacularly brief.

A miscellany of temporary occupations ensued. First, Errol became assistant manager of Kenabot Plantation, a few miles away from Kokopo. Then there were more jobs, unrelated to copra, before he secured the post of manager of Lemus Plantation at Kavieng in New Ireland.

In 1928 he became ill, perhaps having succumbed to the scourge of malaria that was to dog him intermittently for the rest of his life, and he returned to Rabaul, where there were more jobs that fitted no pattern but rootlessness and inconsequence. Even so, Errol achieved the paradox of being shabby but dapper; he already possessed his greatest attribute – style.

Eventually, he and a local character called Dusty Miller were employed on a schooner that was used in the recruitment of native labour. Later, Errol and the schooner were hired by Dr Herman F. Erben for a trip up the unsavoury Sepik River (referred to by Errol as the "Septic" River) to film headhunters. Errol also possibly worked for a time on another schooner, the *Matupi.* It was these periods, lasting several months, and the events that filled them that he presented in highly fictionalized form in his novel *Showdown.*

At this stage, he actually held two jobs at once, possibly because plantation-management did not pay well enough after he had resumed it following his stay in Rabaul.

He decided at last to take a boat back to Kavieng, but there he caught gonorrhoea, and a doctor gave him what was probably "the worst treatment a man could get: a series of applications of permanganate of potash injected into the urethra". Later, Errol was to write: "When my friends learned what I had, I became a sort of hero – but I was terrified."

He had to get back to Sydney. In October 1929, when he was just over twenty years of age, he returned to Rabaul and thence travelled to Sydney.

Whatever opinion one might have formed of the authenticity of his adventures, Errol Flynn at twenty was an experienced young man, extremely personable, possessed of keen wits and rare charm. Though his formal education had been patchy and only a fool would have called him bookish, he had read extensively, even if he sometimes "skipped, muddled and waded". It was probably Aristotle and Plato whom he found hard going, but he read H. G. Wells' *Outline of History,* and not surprisingly for one of such panache, he pronounced himself most influenced by Edmond Rostand – read in French. (As an actor, he never played the title-role in *Cyrano de Bergerac,* but he would have acquitted himself well, especially in the more extrovert aspects of the part.)

For books he often had plenty of time, since the nocturnal hours on a plantation or in the New Guinea jungle were not filled with urban distractions. From Sydney, Professor Flynn would send him parcels of magazines and books, which, when they arrived after two weeks or more, Errol would fondle with sensuous delight. By the light of a hurricane-lamp, competing with "every goddamned bug in the jungle", he would dip into books voraciously and with catholic interest. Two titles mentioned in connection with the hero of *Showdown* give us some idea of other favourites besides Rostand: Hakluyt's *Voyages* and Gauguin's *Private Journals.* At least through reading, he also flirted with communism. At one time, having studied the lives of great lawyers in England and the United States, he turned his thoughts to law, in which his fine voice, he believed, would be ideal for forensic eloquence. He actually went as far as writing to his father informing him that he intended to go to Cambridge and read for the Bar.

These literary tastes are worth dwelling upon if only to correct any impression that his existence so far had been one long picaresque comedy. He did not become a heavy drinker until later. Indeed, it has been said that he was careful to keep his head clear for poker, at which, he asserted, he won £400, a lot of money in those days, on the very eve of his return to Sydney. Venereal disease gives us some indication of his sex-life, and though certain episodes in it might be doubted (then and later), it was undeniably vigorous and even questing, exploratory in its way. "The most vital thing in life," Errol wrote, "is to be able to understand about it."

Recuperating, he remained in Sydney for about six months, during which he and Naomi Dibbs became more deeply attracted to each other. He had various jobs and said he was earning a living by modelling suits – actor's work of a sort. He conceived the idea of buying the *Sirocco,* a ten-ton, forty-four foot cutter-rigged yacht that was nearly fifty years old and had known some success in competitions. Despite its age, the craft was solidly built of ironbark and kauri, though, to quote Errol, "so narrow in the beam that you could lie across her".

By now, Professor and Mrs Flynn were certainly concerned about their drifter of a son (and probably shocked if they knew the nature of his "illness"). Mrs Flynn might also have been worried about the breach between Errol and her. At any rate, she provided the £120 for him to become owner of the *Sirocco,* though precisely how yacht-ownership would make Errol less of a drifter and more responsible is not clear. A career of looking handsome at the helm was possible only for a movie-star, and as yet there were no signs of his becoming one.

By mid-February 1930, the *Sirocco* was ready for a test-run after repairs. Errol was on good terms with Lars Halvorsen, the boat-builder, but left the work partly unpaid for. Halvorsen, a victim of the devastating Flynn charm, forgave him. On trial, there was considerable trouble from the *Sirocco*'s Swedish engine – a timely warning that appears to have gone unheeded or at least not to have been regarded seriously enough.

Several weeks later, the yacht left Sydney for New Guinea after so many abortive departures that friends and relatives finally stopped coming to see the crew off. To put it conservatively, they were an inexperienced bunch – Errol plus his friends Rex Long-Innes, Charlie Burt and H. F. Trelawny Adams.

A contemporary photograph showed a husky-looking bunch, of whom Errol, pipe in mouth, appeared the slimmest and tallest, as well as the most handsome. Rex, long-faced and toothy, had a passing resemblance to Sir Edmund Hillary. Perhaps because of the literary fate he was keeping in store for him, the author of *Beam Ends** builds up Trelawny as the dreamer and idealist of the party. He was a "shy, retiring youth" (he looked the oldest of the quartet and seemed somewhat less than shy as the cruise went on) with whom Errol had been at school in Ireland. (Of course, Errol, when he published in 1937, was working assiduously at the Irish background he and Warner Brothers had concocted.) "He had just graduated from Cambridge University, an engineer with the ability, in theory, to build any sort of bridge you wanted. An aunt had bequeathed him an estate in Tasmania and he had been two months in Sydney trying to collect it. There were so many legal difficulties, however, that at the moment he was in much the same circumstances as myself, broke and jobless. He had, it is true, offered to build the Australians some bridges, but I gathered this had not met with any hysterical enthusiasm." Charlie Burt, fortunately for Errol the writer, had a contrasting pedigree. "He was a young Englishman from the Isle of Man, who had just been sacked from a sheep station in the back country. Hardly surprising, this, for Manx men are sailors, not goatherds. The sea is in their blood, bred there by generations of ancestors who made British naval history. Charlie was short and stocky, wore his hair cropped like a convict and spoke like a judge. In fact, his whole attitude was judicial and solemn. If he asked you to pass the salt you immediately wanted to get counsel's advice first. He wandered aboard one day, introduced himself, and said he had once been a half-owner of the *Sirocco.* He and his partner had been forced by lack of funds to sell her to the ship yard where I had bought her."

If that last part was true, it did not prevent Charlie's having as little idea of how to sail the yacht as the rest of his new-found companions.

As some indication of what a foolhardy venture this 3,000-mile voyage was, the trip to New Guinea, supposed to take six weeks, lasted seven months, though not all the delays were attributable to amateur seamanship. The *Sirocco* arrived at Port Moresby in September 1930, the main hold-ups having been caused by inexperience, the temperamental engine –

*By Errol Flynn; published 1937.

and the life-style of the mariners, which included large measures of carousing and wenching.

The only detailed account of the voyage, a not too reliable one, was set down by Errol in the mid-'thirties in his book *Beam Ends*. Ports of call appear to have included Port Stephens, Coff's Harbour, Ballina and then Brisbane, where, having done much the same for two weeks at Ballina, the young men spent seven days drinking, playing poker and chasing girls. Errol, however, did overhaul the unpredictable engine – a task that occupied a great deal of his time and immensely taxed his patience. ("I spent twenty-four hours taking the engine down and did the job so thoroughly that it took me forty-eight to get it together again.")

The rough seas to Port Stephens, two hundred miles north at the end of the first leg of their journey, had made a bad start, if their ignominious departure from Sydney had not been one already. The four tyro-sailors had not been prepared for such an initiation. "I was soaked to the skin," wrote Errol, "as the ship suddenly dived into the first large head swell. Another came on top of it, and we went under that one, too.

"All attempts to make some hot coffee were hopeless. No sooner was a kerosene stove lit than a sea would come over and buckets of water pour through the leaking forward hatch to put it out. Besides you had to hold the pot on the stove. If you left it for a second it would be on the floor. Holding the pot on the stove meant staying in the galley and staying in the galley meant being horribly seasick. Even on deck still meant being horribly seasick, but the galley seemed to hold a soul-destroying variety of its own. Rex was the only one who still fought against it.

"With an affected nonchalance he was making desultory jokes, but his face was turning green and his jokes becoming more and more ghastly."

To add to their troubles, with every plunge of the *Sirocco*, they could hear crashes from below that did not exactly inspire confidence.

But at last they reached Port Stephens, where Rex reported "a deplorable lack of daughters among the fisherfolk".

Their incalculably slow progress had one consequence that

they had never dreamed of. While they were having fools' luck and enjoying good fellowship with local characters at their various ports of call, strangers were worrying about them – a fact that Errol later attempted to shrug off with literary insouciance: "I have omitted to mention that while safely anchored in Richmond River, vessels up and down the coast were keeping a lookout for our bodies. We were reported lost at sea. Having set sail for Brisbane, when we failed to show up there the harbour authorities had posted us missing. They knew that if we had called at any intermediate port it would have been reported immediately in the shipping news. The fact that we were not so reported was due to the pilot [at Ballina], congenial fellow, having forgotten all about it in the festivities of our arrival."

The voyage thus far had been a mixture of the frivolous and the terrifying. Instead of a week, as Errol had calculated, it had taken them a month to get from Sydney to Brisbane, where they decided to stay for at least seven days to get the engine properly overhauled. According to Errol, Brisbane in summer was a hot, uncomfortable city, its oppressiveness in no degree relieved by the way the sober citizens went around dressed in unsuitably dark, heavy clothes.

Trelawny, anxious to wear a pith helmet that had been purchased in Sydney, was treated to ridicule by street-urchins. He retreated to the *Sirocco,* his helmet wrapped up in a parcel.

If Trelawny's shyness extended even more acutely to women, Rex compensated with a rare boldness. Nor did that boldness wither before females who were not altogether beautiful and not entirely defenceless.

"Opposite our mooring," Errol related, "the Brisbane Ladies' Rowing Club had their boatshed. With his unequalled nerve, Rex went over there one day and appointed himself club trainer. We could see him seated comfortably on the stern of the skiff being rowed all over the river by four sweating girls." He brought them back to the *Sirocco* for tea, and close up, if he had not realized it before, Errol saw that "rowing is no sport for ladies wanting to preserve their figures. Each one of the girls could have earned her living in a sideshow. They had great difficulty getting down the com-

Errol and Olivia de Havilland in *Captain Blood*

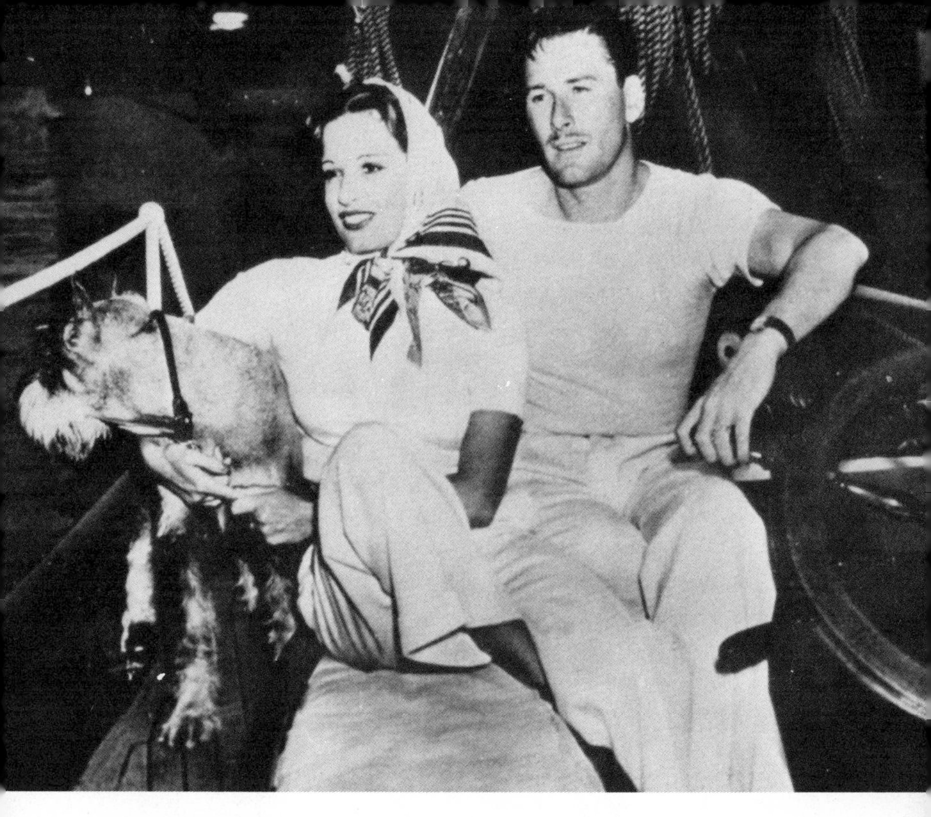

Errol and Lili Damita with the famous Arno on the *Sirocco*

Errol and Lili (1937)

On the set of *The Sisters*: Errol and Bette Davis

Errol and his schnauzer, Arno

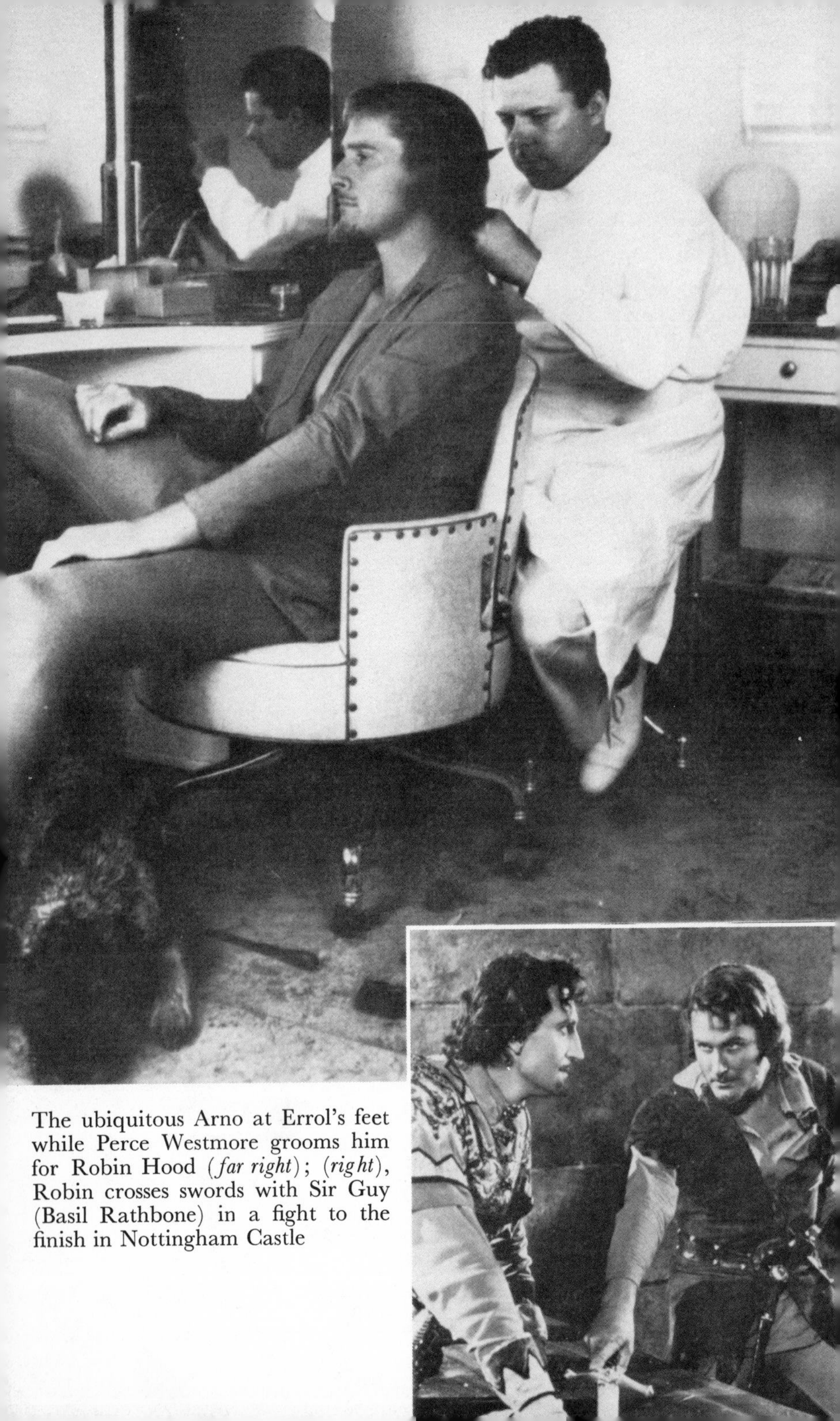

The ubiquitous Arno at Errol's feet while Perce Westmore grooms him for Robin Hood (*far right*); (*right*), Robin crosses swords with Sir Guy (Basil Rathbone) in a fight to the finish in Nottingham Castle

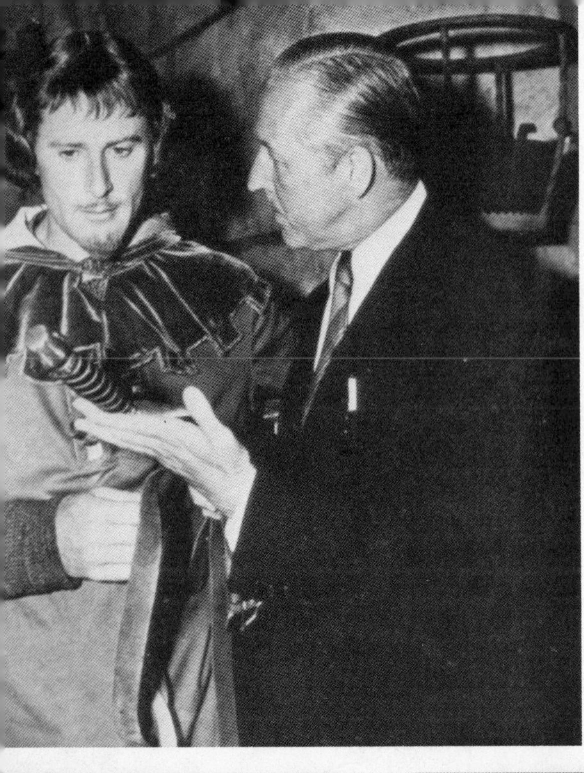

Errol and William Keighley discuss a scene from *Robin Hood*

The Dawn Patrol: David Niven returns in style from the dead

panionway into the cabin and once there, quite overflowed it." Some hyperbole undoubtedly went into this description, but the girls themselves perhaps spoke no more than the truth when they said that their sport kept them superbly fit.

There being no competition, Rex invited the smallest of the group, "an ethereal little thing of some two hundred pounds", to go with him to the cinema.

"He came back late," Errol commented, "and in silence began to apply iodine to several large black abrasions on his body.

"We watched him interestedly. 'Get run over?' I asked.

" 'No,' he answered shortly.

" 'I see. Just tried a bit of gorilla stuff on [your date], eh?'

"Rex replaced the stopper in the bottle and put it back in the medicine chest. He felt the back of his head tenderly.

" 'You may not believe this,' he said. 'That woman threw me five yards through the air!' "

After Brisbane, with better weather, a more confident crew and the establishment of a routine, things improved. The four called in at Bundaberg, where they were caught up in the annual carnival and delayed by Rex's involvement with a local barmaid. When, attempting a shortcut, they ran the *Sirocco* on to mud banks on the voyage between Bundaberg and Rockhampton, they spent hours playing poker until the tide lifted them clear.

Before that, however, Errol had had his moment of pugilistic glory at Bundaberg. Curly Bell, who owned the rodeo-show that was part of the carnival celebrations, offered five pounds to anyone who could stay in the ring for five rounds with one Jack Cowper, the Heavyweight Champion of the Western Districts. Urged on by his friends and as greedy for the money as they were on his behalf, Errol took up the challenge. He noted: "Curly was surprised and suspicious. He probably suspected I might be some professional fighter out for a bit of easy money, but then he must have decided I did not look like one for he smiled and offered me a pair of dirty shorts . . . I declined these in the toughest and most contemptuous manner I could manage."

Cowper took Errol by surprise. Dispensing with the usual

courtesies, he ignored his young opponent's proferred hand and almost finished the fight immediately by knocking him flat. Errol hung on to the end of the round, after which, eager for revenge, he missed Cowper's chin at the beginning of the second but opened up a gash over the man's eye with the lacing on his glove. Egged on by the crowd, Errol put up a good enough show for the champion, alarmed by the sight of his own blood, to retire at the end of the round.

But if Captain Flynn was up at Bundaberg, he was down but not out at Rockhampton, where he greeted the local press from his bunk, to which he had repaired with a bout of malaria. Two days later, however, he was fit enough to join up with his friends in the Rockhampton Carnival. For three weeks, they were swept up in a blur of alcohol, circus performers and chorus girls. (There are, in the usual Flynn manner, conflicting accounts of the Rockhampton weeks in *Beam Ends* and *My Wicked, Wicked Ways,* but the high jinks described in both books certainly took place, though even the names of those involved do not match in the two versions.)

It was a giant called Johnson who had interviewed Errol in his bunk. An ex-professional boxer, he was enormous, dirty, untidy and battered – an ugly brute of a man. His friend Brody, another journalist on the staff of the *Rockhampton Graphic,* was the opposite – small and quite the dandy. As reporters, these two gained free admission everywhere. Brody was "an irrepressible liar" – high praise from Errol; and he used Johnson's might to protect himself from the consequences of his insulting manners. This couple were responsible, directly or indirectly, for most of the high-spirited fun that eventually landed Errol behind bars – where he at least had Brody for company. Johnson, the victim of the same brawl in which Errol ran foul of the law, paid a stiffer price and ended up in hospital.

Exhausted by their escapades, Errol and his crew took life easy drifting among the islands of the Great Barrier Reef, on one of which, Percy Island, they found a superabundance of turtles, with which they had fun and games. He described the interlude thus: "It was the egg-laying season and we would find females in the early morning ponderously waddling back to the water after laying a clutch of two hundred or more round white eggs like golf balls. Turtle riding is a lot of fun. Long ago the statement of de Rougement in his chronicles that the coastal waters of Australia were inhabited by great turtles half the size of a ship's boat, on the backs of which the aborigines rode for sport, was hailed with laughter as the journalism of a sensationalist.

"But we had many a race. You get on the female's back and hold her at front and rear. She puts down her head and starts for the waters of the lagoon. On the beach the going is easy, but once your mount enters the water, it is a different matter. At first you find you have to let go and rise to the surface as soon as she dives, but after a while you learn the knack of holding your steed's head up in a certain way so that she is unable to dive, and then comes the real fun of turtle riding. The excited animals swim about the surface of the lagoon clumsily trying to unseat you and you can steer in any direction you wish."

The description may make the sport sound somewhat cruel, and perhaps it was, though throughout his life Errol had a fondness for domestic pets, and he was later, after seeing what happened during the making of *The Charge of the Light Brigade,* to complain to the Society for the Prevention of Cruelty to Animals about the treatment of the horses.

On another island, the voyagers from the *Sirocco* found a different, more alluring diversion. They ran across the Wilson family, whose twenty-year-old daughter Lucy was a gorgeous child of nature. Stunned by the first sight of her, Errol discovered that she was "even more beautiful at close quarters. She had no make-up of any sort, but intense excitement had given her cheeks a wonderful glow and, dressed only in a white frock, without shoes or stockings, she looked like some pagan virgin of ancient times". She and Errol went for long walks on the beach in the moonlight. One day, she impetuously threw off her dress and plunged into a mountain stream. He was tempted, but he restrained himself – "I stood on the bank, tortured, knowing it was no use; knowing how childlike innocence disarms and that for me there could be no plucking of the lotus."

When the *Sirocco* left, Lucy swam after the yacht and climbed on board, presumably with the intention of following Captain Flynn to the ends of the earth. The four held council about what to do with her, and when Rex, the other Great Lover of the bunch, poked fun at Errol, there was a fight, during which he decked Rex. At last, commonsense prevailed, they bundled her up in a blanket, and Lucy was left sobbing on the beach.

Again, and possibly in reaction to the stress, Errol had an attack of malaria, serious enough this time for the yacht to put in at Townsville, where he spent three days in hospital.

When they reached Cairns, a Chinaman rejoicing in the name of Gabriel Aloysius Achun commissioned them to help him with some opium-smuggling – an episode to which Errol devoted some twenty pages of *Beam Ends.* Eventually, Achun tried to swindle them of the thirty pounds he had offered for their co-operation, but the four balanced the books to their satisfaction by later stealing his dinghy – thus making a small profit.

There were to be more adventures before the *Sirocco* reached Port Moresby, chief among them a magnificent brawl erupting from a fan-tan game at Cairns; an encounter between Rex and a shark while he was swimming; a trip overland to the tobacco-growing centre, Mareeba; and more rough seas.

Despite the last, a climax to the voyage which they could no doubt have done without, they did at last reach Port Moresby in one piece, but when Errol came to write *Beam Ends,* this big finish was not enough: two days out of Port Moresby, he decided to write, "tragedy struck and struck hard" as a hurricane smashed the *Sirocco* to bits on a reef.

As if this lie were not sufficient, the author decided to kill off Trelawny Adams – "Dook", as the others had come to call him. "Kindly, lovable old Dook", he was "too fine and decent a spirit to be cut off so young", and his body was never found. (Hale and hearty, he became a schooner-captain and was later Errol's partner in the tobacco-business.) This literary flourish scarcely did Errol much good, since the tale was occasionally to pop up in his later life as evidence of his cowardice: he left his friend to drown when the boat was swamped. "It is of such stuff," as John Hammond Moore aptly remarks, "that legends are made."

Moore, whose attitude is that the whole of *Beam Ends* must be treated with alert scepticism, dismisses the last two chapters as pure fiction. He admits, however, that the *Sirocco* did end up on a reef, but not in the manner described by Errol or with such disastrous consequences either to yacht or crew.

On 10th December, Errol and Rex put out to sea with a Port Moresby barmaid (they were obviously very big with barmaids), and the unreliable engine acted up again. Although the yacht ended up on the reef, it was salvaged and repaired. Errol lived to read his own obituary several years later after an excursion to the Spanish Civil War, but he penned the *Sirocco*'s himself.

On 7th January 1931 Errol and Rex returned to Sydney on the *Morinda,* arriving a week later. Two weeks afterwards, his engagement to Naomi Dibbs was announced, and an efflorescence of social life ensued for the next three months before Errol, again on the *Morinda,* returned to Port Moresby on 30th April. He had been bitten by the urge for a fast buck, and tobacco looked a likely prospect. With several backers, some of whom (the Flynn charm again) clearly adored him, Errol purchased a five-acre plantation near Rouna Falls on the Laloki River not far from Port Moresby. There was talk of quick profits to be made in the tobacco-trade, but he was not to find them. Nevertheless, he and his labourers probably worked fairly hard during the turn of the year 1931–2.

Even so, the venture was not a success, perhaps because the curing-process was faulty but also because Errol could not sell any of his crop in Australia owing to unfavourable tariffs – a subject on which he wrote pointedly to the *Bulletin,* Australia's foremost weekly.

My Wicked, Wicked Ways contains a story of how Errol, to promote his enterprise, took eight garishly dressed Papuans to Sydney, where one of them, Anitok, ran amok in Anthony Hordern's department store. The anecdote, hard to accept as anything but fiction, is worthy of mention because Anitok appears as one of the chief characters in the novel *Showdown*. Errol was never one to give up on a good literary idea.

Since he could not sell his tobacco in Australia, planter Flynn shipped it off to England, and in late July he sailed to Sydney, arriving there on 5th August 1932.

This, though he could have known it only in retrospect, was the turning point of his life.

If he had stayed in that part of the world continuing the sort of life he had been leading, Errol himself knew that there was a real danger of his becoming a bum. It is not difficult to construct a scenario for what would have happened to him. Without a job offering status and a reasonable salary, he would have become a local character, the subject of many tales told both by himself and by others. His drinking would undoubtedly have increased, as would his brawling. There would have been several brushes with the law, not excluding some serious ones. Perhaps some vengeful husband would have taken a shot at this threat to the marital state. Though he was to age prematurely in Hollywood, he would surely have died early or declined swiftly in Australia and New Guinea – a victim of disease, dissipation or some stupid accident; possibly all three.

If the theorizing sounds too fanciful, consider the predispositions of his character. There had been thus far little stability in his life. (The evidence suggests neglect as a child, though no deliberate cruelty: Professor Flynn was preoccupied with his work, while Marelle, absent from her son for much of the time, was arguably not the sort of woman who should have had children.) Regardless of his engagement to Naomi, it was not in Errol's nature to marry and settle down, as later history made abundantly clear. He had shown no application in his work, but he had a strong inclination towards drink, gambling and casual sex. Both his life and his lies displayed a definite bias towards the illicit and the illegal. He had established a pattern of rootlessness and instability that he never really escaped in his career as a filmstar. Such stability and self-discipline as he possessed manifested themselves only uncertainly, in flashes. On paper at least, he was totally devoid of qualifications.

Errol knew all that and was sensitive enough to fear the outcome if he did not quit that part of the globe and find some remotely congenial – and remunerative – employment.

But, as Berlioz said of Meyerbeer, he had not only the luck to be talented, but also a remarkable talent for being lucky; and it was about to pay off in a big way for the first time. That his talent as an actor happened to be latent, undiscovered so far, did not make it any the less real, as events were to show.

Back in Sydney, Errol's great moment came. He was spotted by John Warwick, a casting director for Cinesound Studios, who was strongly impressed by his physique and handsomeness and knew that Charles Chauvel, a famous Australian moviemaker, was looking for someone to play Fletcher Christian in a film about the *Bounty.* Though Warwick did nothing at the time, presumably waiting until he had had a word with Chauvel, he later found out the name of the striking young man he had seen at the beach near Bondi and arranged for Errol and the producer and his wife to meet.

(In *My Life With Charles Chauvel,* Elsa Chauvel recalled that Errol seemed the perfect Fletcher Christian, but she and her husband were worried about his acting-ability. With impudent grin, Errol said, "I'll try anything once." He captured the studio – if not the movie-going public; and it was hard to keep the girl cutters off the set and in the cutting-rooms.)

The result was Errol's first screen-role, in Chauvel's *In the Wake of the Bounty.* Filming took place from September to November of 1932, during which time Errol was involved for approximately three weeks. In the conventional sense, he had no technique and little idea of what he was supposed to be doing, but he had the natural bearing many professionals strove hard to attain as well as looks that could atone for great holes in his histrionic ability. The Chauvels and their photographer, Tasman Higgins, had shot footage on Pitcairn Island and Tahiti, and this they married with studio-bound sequences that were made in Sydney. Thus any account by Errol that he filmed in Tahiti for *In the Wake of the Bounty* is utterly false. His scenes took place mainly in Captain Bligh's quarters, and he had little to do except 'react' to the captain's tirades. Even so, though hampered by a blonde wig, he turned in a creditable performance, so that not only hindsight makes his acting seem the most convincing in the cast.

The film had yet to be shown by mid-November, when Errol was living in a flat in the King's Cross district of Sydney, and in fact by the time it was premièred, he was out of Australia and on his way to England.

But not without one more amorous adventure that he combined with a genuine crime.

Having made his screen-début in one of the "only two actors' wigs in Sydney", Errol found it impossible to get further work in films. With the outlook bleak, he held his head "higher than ever" – a characteristic that might have helped to impress Madge Parks (if that was her name – it seems unlikely), whom he met at this time, according to him somewhere near Usher's Hotel or possibly inside it when Errol was "snitching more than [his] fair share of cheese and ham and bread at the counter".

He implies in *My Wicked, Wicked Ways* that she picked him up. She was "statuesque, auburn-haired, married, rich, charming, sophisticated", and she was almost twice his age. Not that the disparity bothered Errol, who said afterwards that he agreed with Kinsey that a woman's sexual prime began at thirty-five. (If so, his later life was curiously filled with young girls who had yet to attain the "height of their sexual tempo".) The sexual demands of Madge Parks, however, taxed even Errol severely, much as he enjoyed trying to keep pace with them, and one night, temporarily exhausted, full of thoughts about his poverty and her affluence, he staggered to the bathroom and returned to be hypnotized by the sight of her jewels on the dressing-table. Madge was asleep, and her jewels (or diamonds; for such they rapidly became two paragraphs later in *My Wicked, Wicked Ways)* were irresistibly enticing. Succumbing, Errol scooped them up and ran off through the streets with them, having stealthily dressed first.

Despite pangs of conscience and telling himself that the diamonds were "only a loan", he cunningly hid them in the hollow handle, designed to take a shaving stick, of his shaving-brush. Concealment, though, offered little real security, so that he decided to get out of town. Even after he had boarded a north-bound steamer, he was not safe, as he found out. Before the boat could leave Sydney, two plainclothes men boarded it and searched his belongings. They found nothing, and Errol bluffed it out, taunting them until they departed.

In Errol's account, he left the ship at Brisbane, having decided that his chance to make a "big kill" lay only in New Guinea. He lacked ready cash, and so he started to walk across Queensland with the long-term hope of hopping a freighter to the north coast of Australia.

In the interior, he took a job well-digging at Diamond Downs. This lasted for two months until he found employment at a sheep-station "in one of the most desolate parts of Australia" – doing, it must be added, one of the most unaesthetic jobs in Australia or anywhere else. On an assembly-line for sheep shearing, Errol had to "dag the hogget" – the "hogget" being a young lamb. In *My Wicked, Wicked Ways,* the author provides the reader with full – and nauseating – details of the process, which he sums up by saying, "All I had to do was stick my face into [a] gruesome mess and bite off the young sheep's testicles." Strong teeth and an even stronger stomach ensured that he stuck to this activity, which paid big money.

And had fringe-benefits.

The sheep-rancher had two daughters, both beautiful, who came home from school for a vacation. Pausing only to clean himself up, Errol made a rapid conquest of the elder daughter that got him into her bed and out of his job. The rancher discovered them and ran for his shotgun. Errol decided the moment had come to be moving on.

Riding the rails, he made more progress (with another girl – "Sheila, the daughter of the hotelkeeper" – to console him in one of the towns he passed through) until he reached Townsville, where, with news that he had won half a gold-claim in a government ballot, he boarded a boat for Salamaua, the port that led to the goldfields.

Recruiting twenty-two native 'boys' by a trick, Errol made his expedition to the New Guinea goldfields, in which he panned for two full weeks without success. He was impatient, of course. But he was also realistic. He and his boys had torn up the sixty-by-sixty-foot claim until it looked as though it had been hit by a huge bomb.

It was then, worried both by the Madge Parks affair and his questionable method of recruiting Kanakas, that he decided to quit. There is some evidence that he left a red-herring to divert the authorities if they should come looking for him – a suggestion that he was travelling to China.

How Errol *really* spent this last phase of his life in Australia and New Guinea is a mystery that this author does not intend attempting to unravel. But it is amazing that he managed to accomplish so much in so short a time. Again and again, simple mathematics and geography tend to contradict his account.

Once more, the safe course is merely to say that there is some truth in his story and some literary exaggeration.

Even if he did not fully realize the fact himself, Errol was severing his connections when he left Sydney, putting a full stop to the life he had been leading. He told himself, even before the theft, that his engagement with Naomi Dibbs was negated by his shameful affair with Madge, who had, after all, seduced him. But the word 'seduced' seems to lack force in this context. Errol had, his previous life suggested, been a willing partner, and if the affair made him unfit to be Naomi's fiancé, then he was probably morally disqualified before he ever entered into the engagement and would certainly have been, with or without Madge, soon after it.

(In his autobiography, he reprinted a letter to his father that might, both date and context suggest, have been bogus. Nevertheless, it contained these revealing words about his engagement: "Although I didn't [propose] the married state I just allowed things to drift that way.")

Other factors were at work. If they had ever seemed better, Errol's prospects were once again worse. He could see that there would be no follow-up to his début in *In the Wake of the*

Bounty, which was not to be a box-office hit, even in its country of origin. But that outlook probably worried him less than the idea of marriage, whatever his feelings for Naomi. In fact, failure gave him a *convenient* reason to break off the engagement, but theft, in a sense, made his future simpler still: so urgently was his departure from Sydney indicated that he lacked time even to explain to Naomi that they could not be married.

In other words, if we take Errol's story of 'Madge Parks' to be true, his new-found morality told him that he had betrayed Naomi and could never marry her. Additionally, the theft of the diamonds simultaneously made it possible for him to skip town without explanations to Naomi and the Dibbs family and forced him, for fear of the long arm of the Australian police, to seek a new life rather than lounge about Sydney. What was necessary was convenient and vice versa. The episode with the detectives made it clear that Mrs Parks or her husband had already complained to the police and that they had Errol lined up as a prime suspect. (What the theft of the jewels did to the Parks marriage can only be imagined.)

On 30th December, Errol arrived in Port Moresby, and by the middle of January he had sold the Laloki tobacco plantation. He then sailed on to Salamaua in New Guinea, and there is evidence that by 10th February he had somehow reached the Edie Creek goldfields and was a goldminer there, perhaps much as he described in his autobiography. If so, it was for a few days only, the explanation being that he was now on the run and had in any case made up his mind to quit both Australia and New Guinea. He could not get out of his head the saying "that if you spent more than five years in New Guinea you were done for, you'd never be able to get out, your energy would be gone, and you'd rot there like an aged palm". He already knew firsthand what malaria could do to a man.

He journeyed to Rabaul, which he probably left on 21st February 1933, if so reaching Manila on 1st March and arriving in Hong Kong three days later.

What happened between then and Errol's arrival in England – a period of a few months at most – is the subject of much speculation and some of the most luridly improbable passages in *My Wicked, Wicked Ways.*

As a source of information about Errol's early life in Australia and New Guinea, *My Wicked, Wicked Ways* is, like almost any other Flynn account, a crazy patchwork, a blur in which truth and falsehood or bad memory frequently diverge. To quote a few examples thoroughly explored by John Hammond Moore in *The Young Errol,* Flynn states that he was a slave-trader on a ship called the *Maski* (Papuan for 'Don't Care' or 'Screw Yourself'); but the colour in this story fades when it is realized that the *Maski* does not appear in any contemporary shipping-lists and that, although he did recruit black labour, this activity was a good deal more respectable – not to say invaluable and esteemed – than Errol later liked to admit in his anecdotes.

The excursion up the Sepik River became curiously linked, at least in the mind of the writer Errol, with his role in Chauvel's *In the Wake of the Bounty.* According to *My Wicked, Wicked Ways,* the unlisted *Maski* and her young captain were hired by an American named Joel Swartz (and not by Dr Herman F. Erben*) to film the headhunters. Errol was a little alarmed if also flattered by this commission, because the Sepik was a "human graveyard", an unexplored river beyond four days by boat. He survived the trip, however, returning to speak of poisoned darts and crocodiles.

Later, after the cruise of the *Sirocco* had ended at Port Moresby, Errol's friends, if the reader were to believe the autobiography, *immediately* returned to Australia. (It will be remembered that Errol and Rex stayed on to sail the *Sirocco* on to a reef.) Errol himself promptly sold the boat and with the proceeds started a tobacco plantation, whence he was summoned by a telegram from the previously mentioned Joel Swartz, who wanted him to play Fletcher Christian in *In the Wake of the Bounty.* The telegram came from Tahiti, whither Errol departed in a flash. But of course we know that he was never in Tahiti for any of Charles Chauvel's – not Swartz's – film-making.

*See page 27.

We must presume that the Joel Swartz of both the novel *Showdown* and the supposedly factual *My Wicked, Wicked Ways* was Dr Herman F. Erben, a specialist in tropical diseases, explorer and anthropological moviemaker. But the complications make the head swim. Joel Swartz appears in the fictional *Showdown,* based on the trip up the Sepik River, though the narrative naturally contains a great deal of invention and artistic transmogrification. But the same mysterious figure pops up as *both* Joel Swartz and Dr Gerrit H. Koets in *My Wicked, Wicked Ways.* Why, it must be asked, did Errol often use real names in the novel and yet change those same names in the autobiography?

Such confusions apart, the New Guinea portions of *My Wicked, Wicked Ways* are a kaleidoscope of vivid events, unforgettable characters and daring, if not rash, deeds.

Not the least of the unforgettable characters are the inevitable Flynn girls.

The first of them appears predictably as soon as Errol has become a cadet at Rabaul. He had a passionate affair, it is stated, with a half Melanesian-Polynesian girl with whom he spent much of the time swimming when they were not presumably engaged in more ardent activities. Unfortunately, the girl, Maura, was unhappily married to a prominent government official, who one night was inconsiderate enough to walk in on their naked dalliance. Between Errol and the irate husband, there was a vicious struggle, which ended when Errol, who as an Australian fought dirty, gave his opponent what he called "the old boot". (Since he was wearing no clothes at the time, he did not mean this expression literally.)

True or not, the episode is nonetheless a colourful illustration of what might be taken for a fact – the young cadet's sexual precocity. More than one mother must have breathed freely at the thought that the handsome Flynn was no longer in Sydney, perhaps Mrs R. Campbell Dibbs (Naomi's mother) among them.

Later, at Laloki plantation, he bought himself a young native girl who became his mistress. She wore a grass skirt and had small but proud breasts. When Errol first saw her, he could only stare and gulp – "I knew I had to buy her." Though at first sulky at being sold into virtual slavery, she gradually responded to his wooing, and they enjoyed an idyllic spell – swimming in the nude, making love and, since neither knew the language of the other, communicating by gestures and touch.

These two, Maura and his companion of the long nights at Laloki, are among the first of the long parade of girls that appear in the pages of *My Wicked, Wicked Ways* – a veritable United Nations, as though Errol were determined to show that he would bed with any attractive woman, regardless of race, class or creed.

The two chapters in his New Guinea sex-life cited here, one might guess, were fact or based on fact.

However, there were two non-sexual episodes, both undoubtedly fictional, that were supposed to have involved the young Flynn at this period and that were cut out of later editions of the autobiography. The first was the account of a punitive expedition led by Cadet Flynn after natives had killed four prospectors near Madang on the northern coast of New Guinea. After a long and exciting journey, Errol and his native police met up with a district officer and his patrols at the scene of the atrocity. Summary justice by hanging was administered to the offenders, and Errol, though he himself was repelled, described the reaction of the natives – hilarity – to the spectacle of the dangling bodies. Though pure fiction as recounted by the author of *My Wicked, Wicked Ways,* this story was at least suggested by an actual event, the famous Nakani Massacre that took place a year before Errol arrived in Rabaul.

Who can doubt that he heard stories about this happening, the talk of the region at the time, and thought them so striking that he incorporated them, suitably rehashed, into reminiscences of his life in Rabaul? Probably a good many folk had heard the gruesome anecdote by the time Flynn decided to set it down in permanent form (as he thought then) in his autobiography.

The second apocryphal chapter has sometimes appeared in books and articles eager to denigrate Errol Flynn, though he had only himself to blame for this carelessly unforeseen consequence. Errol had been, he wrote, to the Sepik River district for the illegal acquisition of bird-of-paradise plumes, which were then greatly in demand. Worried about his illicit activity, he decided to return to Salamaua before the law caught up with him. By an irony worthy of fiction (which is precisely what this episode turned out to be), he was there arrested on a charge of murder. During an ambush, he had fired at a group of natives, one of whom had died. Errol proved equal to the occasion. It is surprising, in view of the circumstances, that he did not enter a plea of self-defence, but having eloquently mentioned in an address to the court that he had been fighting for his life, he settled, in the manner of a television lawyer, for a technicality of law: the prosecution, he challenged, could not produce the *corpus delicti.* He was right, and as a result he was acquitted.

The tale made good reading, but it was exposed as a fraud and had to be excised.

Among much else, equally vivid, that may or may not have been true – Errol's escape from a crocodile, the dynamiting of fish, natives playing with sharks "like puppies" – there is an account of how Errol became plantation manager at Kavieng that at least has the ring of truth.

A Chinaman called Ahsims or simply Sims (a fictitious name for a real character – Ah Chee), a saloon-keeper in Rabaul, introduced him to Al Tavisher, Sim's partner in a copra plantation, and it was Tavisher who offered Errol the job. This whole interlude has its clearly autobiographical counterpart in *Showdown,* in which the hero, Shamus, is asked whether he knows anything about running a plantation:

"The look which spread over Shamus's face indicated how inept the question had been. Running a plantation! Why, off and on, it was all he'd been doing for the past ten years, he assured Mr Endersby blandly, although actually the most he knew was looking at one from a distance. The job was his on the spot. But as Mr Endersby left the bar, Shamus lagged behind long enough to whisper to the friendly Irish bartender, 'How do you run a copra plantation?' The bartender winked at him slowly. 'You don't. You bloody well ask the boss boy everything you don't know, and let him run the show for you.' "

Substitute Tavisher for Endersby in the above quotation, and you probably have a fairly accurate account of what actually took place.

When Errol wrote *My Wicked, Wicked Ways,* he described obtaining the job in pretty much the same terms but with a friend called Basil Hoare, "a young Englishman with a first-rate record in World War I as a naval commander", playing the role of "the friendly Irish bartender". Hoare's advice to Flynn was: "Easy, old boy, nothing to it . . . You just get hold of the Boss Boy . . . On every plantation there is a Boss Boy. You call for him and just say to him, 'Boss Boy, carry on!' "

If both accounts were fiction, all one can say is that as an author Errol was to some degree consistent. The point of the anecdote, however described, is that he was learning, if he had not already known it by instinct, how to bluff, how you could always make things look a little better than they were.

Instinct or lesson, he never forgot it.

3

Another Dawn

When Errol realized that "the curtain was coming down on New Guinea" – the words with which he ended Part Two of his autobiography – he had only a vague idea that he was to move fairly soon into a stage-career. His discovery that he could master dialogue for *In the Wake of the Bounty* did not mean that he had been bitten by the acting-bug, even though he had tried to find more work in Australian films. More probably the thought had occurred quite strongly to him that acting was a job for which one did not inevitably need qualifications other than looks and personality (he had proved that); that an actor's life was reasonably congenial; and that he might make it pay the rent.

If he could find a job.

He had no vocation. Lofty notions of scaling the pinnacles of Thespian art, if they ever inspired him, did not strike until much later.

Errol stated that after leaving New Guinea he travelled through seven seas in eight months. During this time, he was constantly in the company of Dr Gerrit H. Koets, whom he met on the boat leaving Rabaul. Koets, a scientist of sorts, was possibly twenty years his senior – "a vast Epstein-like sculpture", according to Errol. He and Koets shared an interest in money, women and experience for its own sake. They also had in common, Errol admitted, "a touch of larceny".

His new friend was a Dutchman, and in the younger partner's words, "Everything about him was broad." He had enormous ears like open taxi-doors, big teeth and hairy legs and thighs. Errol's description also conveys the rather intriguing information that "his face was covered with blond hair, though he wasn't exactly bearded". Koets fancied himself as a womanizer and had a unique way of attracting attention – so arresting that it is surprising that he was not thrown off the ship.

Every morning, he would stand naked at the stern, thrusting his vast chest at the sun and pounding himself gorilla-fashion. Errol reported that there were few passengers on the ship, which was a freighter, but the captain's wife – fortyish and eleven stone, yet not without appeal during a scarcity of women – did not throw herself at Koets as he had led Errol to believe she might.

The two had many adventures that must be regarded with appropriate scepticism. In Manila, where they rented a hut with a mud floor, they hit on an idea to make money through cock-fighting. Using snake-venom, they poisoned the beaks of the birds they had bought, and for a while they lived high on their winnings until the Filipinos began to wonder how two strangers had managed to maintain such a run of luck with such vicious birds. Suspicion became so strong that they had to race for a boat – one jump ahead of the police. Even so, they were comparatively rich.

The next stop was Hong Kong, where Errol and Koets played the horses without much success. It was Errol's idea to move on to Macao, where they would invest the $2,000 remaining to them in fan-tan at one of the casinos. On the *Fusham*, a ferry between Hong Kong and Macao, Errol met Ting Ling O'Connor.

With a name sounding like "the ring of a bicycle bell", she was Chinese on her mother's side, and her father had been a Colonel O'Connor. By eastern standards, she was tall – five-foot-seven, and she had a beautiful profile and figure, the second displayed in a high-collared dress of Mandarin-red with a side-split. While Errol was wondering about how to make an approach to her, she spoke first. Her mother was seriously ill, and Ting Ling was going to Macao to try to make some money through gambling – she and Errol had that much in common.

What more natural than that they should gamble together?

They arranged to meet at the roof casino of Macao's de luxe Mandarin House Hotel, where they seemed to bring each other luck. Both won considerable sums, and afterwards they danced together. Errol escorted her to her room, played the gentleman and left her with a kiss on the hand. As he said goodnight, Ting Ling looked puzzled.

Swimming always played a significant part in Errol's love-life, and when he met her at the seaside next afternoon, he was stunned by her semi-nude loveliness, even though the exposure offered by the bathing suit of those days was far short of that displayed by the later bikini. They swam, lay in the sun and talked, exchanging family histories. If there was a problem, it was that Errol – perhaps uncharacteristically – did not know how to move their relationship beyond this stage of the seemingly social and companionable.

Possibly there were no signals. Maybe he was baffled by the inscrutable East.

Ting Ling resolved the difficulty. On the second night, once they were in her room, she removed her panties – "gay, gossamer, tussah silk, with little quaint designs of dragons embroidered diagonally across them" – and extended a delicate and helping hand to the shy Errol. So exquisite was her art that he became after that night an enthusiast for Chinese culture.

For a week, they were constantly together, and they combined in more than making love and the joys of winning at fan-tan. One night, Ting Ling introduced him to opium. Instead of being taken to the lurid 'den' he had expected, Errol was conducted to a perfectly ordinary room. What took place there, however, was far from ordinary. After Errol had smoked two pellets of opium, he experienced hallucinations and a feeling of being disembodied – yet not, obviously, beyond earthly lusts. He took his beautiful Eurasian mistress to another room, where he amazed himself with his own erotic virtuosity and sexual endurance. He was later told that opiates depressed desire in the male while stimulating it in the female, and yet he himself had proved extraordinarily potent.

To leave the reader uncertain of the authenticity of the tale, he wrote in *My Wicked, Wicked Ways*: "Next day I put it all down to a dream."

He was beginning to wake up to reality, however.

His luck at gambling had begun to turn sour, but he was sure it would change. When he went to her hotel to meet Ting Ling, to whom he had loaned a considerable amount of money, he discovered that she had checked out without leaving any messages. A scornful Koets asserted that the lovely Ting Ling O'Connor had been a confidence trickster also called Yok An Lee, among other aliases. Acting as a shill for the gambling management, she was employed to double the play and break the customer. Undoubtedly, she had picked up Errol on the boat as a strictly commercial proposition.

Well, not *strictly* commercial.

Errol might have been taken, but he did not feel too badly about it. After all, he had been given something, too.

But worse was to follow.

Deciding that the scene had gone cold on them, he and Koets took the boat back to Hong Kong. Errol still had of course the diamonds he had taken from Madge Parks, and having recovered them from the captain's safe-keeping after the ship reached Hong Kong, Errol repaired to the bar, where, groggy with booze and malaria, he struck up a conversation with a fellow Australian who proved his equal in charm.

What took place was predictable.

The boat docked, Errol left, and he stuck his hand in his jacket-pocket, where he had put the diamonds, only to discover that it was empty. He recalled that, turning hot and then cold with malaria, he had taken off his jacket in the bar and hung it on the back of his chair.

He and Koets raced back to the ship to raise a hue-and-cry. They were of course too late.

The diamonds had gone as they had come, and there was a kind of poetic justice in their fate.

The two men had only a few pounds left between them, and it was at this point, if *My Wicked, Wicked Ways* is to be believed, that they joined the Royal Hong Kong Volunteers.

Perhaps, contrary to all appearance, they did. If so, they were sadly disappointed in their expectations – whatever those might have been. They were shipped immediately to

Shanghai, where they were told to dig trenches and did so – with bullets occasionally passing over their heads – "for days". (When he came to write about this excursion, Errol's sense of time, as it so often did, became vague.)

Digging and being shot at were too much for Koets and Errol.

To get out, they needed something called a Shanghai Province Permit. Errol provided it. He added embellishments and adornments to it, but it was essentially a Chinese laundry slip bearing the words in English: "Not responsible for laundry left here over six months."

It did the trick.

The next scene in this drama of romance and adventure found Errol and Koets on a French ship, the *D'Artagnan,* taking them to Ceylon. It would not have been complete without an interlude of amorousness.

This time, the subject of Errol's attentions was Mayako, a delectable Japanese girl whose husband was a Swiss boor. He was taking her back to Switzerland because she was gravely ill, presumably with tuberculosis. If she was going to die, Errol reasoned after seeing her, she deserved one more adventure in love. If she was going to die, she would consciously seek it – and with him.

He was right.

For most of the time, her husband was obligingly absent, but returning at an inopportune moment, he first tried to strangle the half-dressed Errol and then attempted to shoot him. However, Errol distracted his attention and flung himself upon the man, although the gun went off, the bullet ricocheting around the steel walls of the cabin. The Swiss had gone berserk. Even so, Errol succeeded in disarming him and threw away the gun.

They were separated by French ship's officers, who had heard the shot. After such a scandal, Errol was asked to leave the ship in Colombo. When he pointed out to the French that he was not such a bad chap, while the Swiss was nuts, they agreed but said that Mayako's husband had paid *two* first-class passenger fares, and he, Errol, had paid only one.

As he observed, "The French are very practical people."

The adventures were drawing to a close. The incident with the rickshaw-man* happened in India, and it took sixteen stitches to close Errol's wound – plus, perhaps, a liberal pinch of salt to believe in the precise manner of its infliction. After touring brothels in the south of France, where Errol saw offensive sights but found whores, whatever else they were, charming conversationalists, he and Koets at last parted in Marseilles. They had inspected bordellos in many parts of the world, but the queerest – in every sense – had been in Marrakesh in French Morocco. There the customers had included Arab sheiks, for whom attractive boys were provided. Errol did not participate. But, then, he was often similarly inactive in heterosexual establishments. Watching, absorbing, understanding – these, too, were the pleasures of the young man who had spent many solitary hours reading in the jungle at night, miles from anywhere.

Of Koets, he wrote: "This man was the great influence in my life. He showed me in a humorous, bawdy, Rabelaisian, tough, rough way the difference between a man with no soul and a man with one, even though neither of us was sure what a soul was . . . I learned from him to laugh at the worst disasters."

It was just as well. There were to be quite a few disasters.

But not for a while yet.

And when they had occurred, Errol often saw them for what they were only in retrospect.

In the spring of 1933, he reached London with the hope of becoming an actor.

His assets included a masculine beauty that almost literally bowled women over. He moved with a graceful athleticism. Devoid of 'Aussie' twang, he had a fine, light voice. (Incidentally, when he reached Hollywood, he never strove for an American accent – a mistake made at least once by no less an actor than Laurence Olivier, in possibly his greatest screen-performance, in William Wyler's *Carrie.*) He could boast that he had appeared in a film, if only an Australian one.

*See page 24.

There was just one snag: he could not act.

Or rather two snags.

Materially, he had virtually no assets at all.

In typical Flynn fashion, he bluffed his way into the Berkeley Hotel. The Berkeley in itself would have been good enough, but so great was the impression he made that he was installed in the Royal Suite. After two days, however, the management became suspicious, but when Errol, turning in his second convincing performance in England, simulated an attack of appendicitis, they transferred him to an expensive West End nursing-home.

The doctors soon discovered that he was sound in body, though his other malady – insolvency – was worrying Errol. To stifle his cares, he turned his attention to his lovely young nurse. There was a lock on his door, and the couple made good use of it. When Errol confided that he was broke, she told him not to worry, as her father was rich. She would help him.

There was one string to the offer, however. Errol was to stay in the nursing-home – the patient ministering to the nurse.

The arrangement suited him admirably until, after two days, he heard her whispering of marriage. Money had by now been paid into his London account, and so he hurriedly wiped out his debt to his nurse.

Or was it so simple?

She articulated her fears of pregnancy.

But nothing was to detain Errol. He left and earnestly began looking for work in the theatre. All his attempts, including some shamelessly exaggerated self-advertisement, failed. After months, though, his agent at last found him a place in the Northampton Repertory Company, which was not Errol's idea of a theatrical Mecca.

But at least it was a job.

He afterwards swore that he was engaged through yet another bluff. The company needed an extra man for their cricket-team, and Errol pretended that he could fill the vacancy. "Thanks to my ignorance of the game," he wrote, "we lost heavily." (Given his partial education in England and his natural flair for sport, his "ignorance of the game" seems somewhat odd.)

But he was in the theatre, and he began to learn his craft through playing "everything: old maids, old women, chauffeurs, butlers, detectives, burglars". We might doubt the first two items in the lists, but the rest sounds like standard repertory-fare. He also played Shakespeare, but only bit-roles until he was cast as Othello – "the worst Othello in the history of the English stage" (which is indeed a title). Misplacing his knife for the Moor's suicide, he improvised and died of a heart attack. The audience loved it. His Desdemona was Freda Jackson, whom he remembered twenty-five years later if only because her taste for onions and beer lent flavour to their more intimate scenes.

Although he knew that the experience he was acquiring was invaluable, he was impatient for the West End. Recognition would be fine; the money would be even better.

At about this time, his literary urges – arguably stronger than those as an actor – prompted him to write a play, *Cold Rice.* In *My Wicked, Wicked Ways,* he described it as a satire, but the reader might be forgiven for suspecting that any satirical qualities were unintentional. It was about the British Empire of India, and "the central fact of the play", its author wrote, "was its sharp ridicule of womanhood. Women seemed to me so stupid, so fatuous, that I had to express it in dramatic terms".

Was a specific young lady on his mind?

A very junior member of the Northampton Rep., she was pretty, sexy – and hopelessly brainless. For a brief affair, these qualifications were little short of ideal, and Errol made the most of her proximity.

He had begun his career by appearing in the Northampton Rep.'s first pantomime as "a dashing and handsome Prince Donzil" in Margaret Carter's *Jack and the Beanstalk.* In 1934, he was in Ibsen's *A Doll's House* with Freda Jackson, both of them only in supporting roles. He gave "a satisfying and sincere performance" in Eden Phillpott's *Yellow Sands* and was in the same author's *The Farmer's Wife.* As a taste of Shaw, he had a part in *The Devil's Disciple.* (Records might indicate that Peter Rosser – and not Errol – played Othello that year;

but perhaps both, at different times, took a crack at the title-role.)

Eventually, at Stratford-on-Avon, Errol appeared in minor roles (a Roman soldier and an Irish policeman) in John Drinkwater's *A Man's House* and Denis Johnston's *The Moon and the Yellow River.* The productions achieved the desired end – specifically, the West End. For all rep. actors like Errol, there existed the fervent hope that whatever provincial company they worked for would turn out to be but a stepping-stone to the bright lights of London.

Errol saw them – briefly. (The two plays lasted only two weeks, and Errol had been at Northampton for a year and a half, though, as he was later to admit, the time had been a happy and enjoyable one.) The plays were running simultaneously, so that he made nightly dashes between theatres. By day, he was probably seeking film-work.

The theatrical exposure, however, was enough. Errol was spotted by Irving Asher, the head of Warner Brothers in England, and he was signed up for an English production, *Murder at Monte Carlo.*

That, at least, was his version.

Asher related that, by persistence, the young actor secured an interview. (John Hammond Moore relates that Asher's wife, having been impressed by Errol's looks when she spotted him in a waiting-room, persuaded her husband to see him.) Either way, the virtually unknown Flynn was secured for a seven years' optional contract. Enthusiastically, Asher, in a cable to Warners in Burbank in October 1934, described him as "best picture bet we have ever seen". He also labelled him Irish.

Was that Errol's idea or was it a false presumption prompted by the surname?

Within three days, a leading man was needed by Asher for a 'quickie', and Errol, never having been a supporting player, became an instant star – but only technically and in relatively unimportant England, for the film was never shown in the US. Made in November 1934, it was not released until August 1935. As its title indicated, the picture was a murder mystery in which Errol's performance was at best adequate.

As a film, *Murder at Monte Carlo* was no great shakes, but as a beginning for Errol Flynn, it did the trick. With a six-month contract at $150 a week, he was invited to go out to Hollywood.

What could he possibly lose?

4

Green Light

Errol crossed to New York on the *Paris,* because those were the days before jet-planes annihilated distance and at the same time severely limited opportunities for romance. Needless to say, Errol found one on the *Paris,* but the episode with a Russian princess that he described so vividly has the familiar aura of fiction.

By his account, in the midst of an amorous encounter, she belaboured his bare bottom with a hairbrush. Before Errol realized what was happening, his buttocks were bleeding. He beat the fastest of retreats.

However, he had a more pleasant meeting on board with the French actress Lili Damita, whose beauty impressed him but upon whom he seemed to have no complementary effect. As a prelude to marriage, it was an inauspicious encounter.

He was supposed to travel directly to Hollywood, and there is a story that Warner Brothers, already well briefed on his wayward disposition, provided him with limited spending-money and a one-way ticket to ensure his prompt arrival. Even so, Errol jumped train in Chicago, where Warner representatives located him days later. If this story is true, Errol certainly glosses over the facts in his autobiography, in which he writes merely that he travelled by train to Chicago and four days later flew to Hollywood. By then, it was the beginning of 1935.

There are few signs that Errol, having been signed by Irving Asher of Warner Brothers in late 1934, had any accurate perception of the vistas unfolding before him. On the contrary, he shared a fashionably aloof attitude to films that stage-players still affect, but he was a congenital wanderer, and seeing Hollywood would be one more adventure. He therefore approached that adventure with his usual flippancy, and at this stage beneath it there was no serious ambition to extend his range, to consolidate a reputation or to polish a craft about which he really knew little.

He was to make no fewer than three pictures that first year in Hollywood, but he was not immediately put to work, and in the interim he grew restless at being "just a spare wheel on the Warner Brothers lot". He made friends with a kindred spirit, "a fun guy" called Bud Ernst, and also with the then unknown Jerry Wald, who, according to Errol, was instrumental in securing his first assignment. Wald was a friend of Michael Curtiz, who was to direct Flynn in twelve films, and Curtiz picked the new actor for a small role in a Warren William 'B' picture.

It was a strange beginning to one of the most glittering of Hollywood careers.

To put it simply, Errol was to play a corpse in this eighty-minute Perry Mason mystery, *The Case of the Curious Bride.* True, his appearance as the corpse was supplemented (if that is the word) by a second brief sequence in flashback – but with no dialogue. This was not a début likely to arouse much interest, though it is possible that Warner Brothers, keeping a close eye on their new contract player, were already sizing up his ability. After all, the studio had signed him up *without* the usual formality of a screen-test, though Jack Warner had asked all his writers to take a good look at *Murder at Monte Carlo,* which was now available for study and might give an indication of the new boy's potential.

Soon after making *The Case of the Curious Bride,* Errol met Lili Damita again, and this time the warmth of her response was unmistakable, so that they began an affair. (Something else also began during this period, because – the autobiography suggests – Errol made his first experiments that spring with marijuana.) An affair was nothing for this "incorrigibly polygamous man" (the label is Errol's; but he meant "polyerotic"). However, when Errol married Lili on 5th May 1935, there must have been many who were surprised.

Perhaps not least the bridegroom himself.

Errol had known attractive women before, and he was not one to lose his head easily, however much Lili's beauty affected him. Furthermore, they had already begun a series of fights and reconciliations. As he told it, they finally acted on an off-the-cuff suggestion by Bud Ernst that he should fly them to Yuma, where they would be married.

Would Flynn have taken the first plunge into matrimony so casually?

It seems unlikely. This was the man who was to say: "The only real wives I have ever had have been my sailing ships." And: "I have never married. I have been tied up with women in one legal situation after another called marriage, but they somehow break up." He must have had strong positive reasons for marrying Lili, but they blurred all too rapidly with the passing of time. Looking back more than twenty years later. Errol had many charges to level against her – the least of them that she was egocentric and possessive. But he admitted that she was a good sport and a fine cook, and he must have been susceptible in the beginning to her animation and beauty.

The subject of his union with Lili will be returned to later, but one possible explanation for this marriage, as for his others, is that he was aware of the lack of discipline in his life and sought to find stability and order with a wife. Errol had these instincts from time to time, but for a man with his *other* impulses, matrimony offered small hope of a safe harbour or a framework within which he would somehow achieve maturity.

His movie-career was continuing if not exactly picking up. In *Don't Bet on Blondes,* yet another Warren William 'B', Errol played a society playboy, in which brief role he had no chance to do more than look handsome and radiate charm.

Then came *Captain Blood.*

Robert Donat had seemed the most likely choice to play the eponymous buccaneer, but either there were contractual problems or what Errol termed "a long-distance quarrel" – with the result that Donat bowed out and a stylish leading man was needed urgently. The spare wheel on the Warner Brothers lot got his chance. Jack Warner decided to play Flynn, then completely unknown, in this major production. Ever afterwards, Errol, though his feelings about the man were mixed, retained a liking and respect for him, despite their sometimes bitter struggles.

At least one commentator has given the impression that *Captain Blood* was a penny-pinching enterprise, but the description is scarcely accurate. Warners was a cost-conscious studio that sought economy by the clever use of miniatures rather than real ships, and whatever view one takes of the budget, enormous talents were lavished on this rousing tale of adventure and the sea, though at the time perhaps many of those talents came comparatively cheaply.

Opposite Errol, Olivia de Havilland, so often to co-star with him, made one of her first appearances in what was certainly her first big role. Basil Rathbone, as a French pirate, fought the first of two memorable screen-duels with Errol (though the swordplay, staged by the incomparable Fred Cavens, lacked the excitement of later Flynn duels). There were some excellent supporting performances, and Michael Curtiz directed with his characteristic flair and authority if not with quite the distinction he was to attain in *The Sea Hawk* and *Robin Hood,* two later Flynn vehicles. As for the teaming of Errol and Olivia de Havilland, her prim loveliness and his smooth assurance seemed to complement each other perfectly.

On the screen at least, he had found an ideal partner.

There are two ways of regarding Errol's performance. In terms of his experience (or lack of it), it is surprisingly good. As he worked, he gained authority, and Curtiz re-shot some of the early footage after the leading man had found his sea-legs, so to speak. Leaving these peripheral matters aside, a less sympathetic, more objective critic might point out that Errol's acting is little more than attractively competent. Even a fanatical admirer might grudgingly admit that the star was later to do much better.

In a sense, the real star of *Captain Blood* was Erich Wolfgang Korngold, whose score not only bestowed on the film much of its sweep and exhilaration but also is one of the few movie-scores whose qualities endure divorced from their context. Distinguished as a composer in other worlds such as the opera, Korngold was perhaps the greatest genius ever to enter a Hollywood music-department, and the fanfares and lyrical impetus of his music were an integral part of *Captain Blood*'s stirring effectiveness. This was his first original score for a film, though he was to score six more Flynn pictures, and it is doubtful whether Errol, who casually acknowledged debts to directors like Curtiz and Raoul Walsh, ever realized how much his artistic career, both at first and later, owed to Korngold. With the passing of time, Flynn and the composer's music have become inextricably linked in a potent chemistry.

(I am indebted to George Korngold, the composer's son, for the information that although his father and Flynn were never closely acquainted, Erich Korngold and his wife met the star on several occasions at parties, where they discovered Errol to be remarkably shy. As a small boy, George Korngold visited the set of *The Private Lives of Elizabeth and Essex* and saw Flynn in one of his resplendent costumes – an experience that provided an indelible memory.)

In December 1935 *Captain Blood* opened to generally enthusiastic notices, and Warners knew they had a star.

This was the first peak in a screen-career that spanned a quarter of a century and took in approximately sixty films, the best of them presenting, to a whole generation of cinemagoers, the most stylish romantic hero of them all.

Let us make a brief digression at this point to look at the subsequent history of that career and the qualities of Errol Flynn that made it possible.

Captain Blood stands the test of time remarkably well, though Errol's performance ranges unequally from the merely passable to the impressively sincere and exhilaratingly dashing. To the discerning eye, though, despite the sequences in which he shone, Flynn lacked experience and was modestly equipped in a technical sense. Even so, his natural endowments were formidable and amounted to the oft-cited but elusive – or at least ill-defined – 'star-quality': it ensured that the attention of the audience was on Errol throughout every scene in which he appeared.

From the beginning, he had a unique screen-presence. He was six-feet two-inches tall, impossibly handsome, with eyes that were always fascinating, and, for most of his career, a thin line of moustache that, despite changes in fashion, he was to shave off only for brief periods. Though it was not his first film, *Captain Blood* conferred instant stardom upon him partly because it *was* his first considerable costume-romance, and his success was largely attributable to the ease and flair with which he wore period-clothes. Nora Eddington, his second wife, said that he was a poor dancer who looked good on the dance-floor because of his height and bearing. Certainly no camera ever captured Errol in a gauche or awkward movement. He had a light, unemphatic yet masculine voice that was like no other. At the beginning of *The Sea Hawk,* Flynn, off-camera, issues a nautical command, and there is no mistaking the tones – they are an impressive harbinger of his first appearance. The accent was a singular one, made up of all sorts of sounds, but definitely, to American ears, an English accent.

But the flawless Flynn physiognomy was without doubt the strongest first and last impression of the actor. These impeccably sculpted features, ideally photogenic, carried more than a hint of the nobility – not to say hauteur – that was to be in most of his famous roles. If there was any note of arrogance, it was softened or at least modulated by an irresistible grin that revealed perfect teeth as well as a rather impudent sense of humour. There was a slight, enviable cleft to his chin that was just right – classical but virile. As if all that were not enough, his eyes spectacularly dominated the face. Their twinkle affected every movie-goer, whether he was conscious of that effect or not; but it was said by those who knew Errol that one characteristic of those eyes eluded the camera and did not translate to the screen. His eyes were brown, but they contained minute gold flecks that appeared to sparkle when he was angry and to radiate warmth when his mood was more agreeable. His hair, often grown long for his parts, was lustrously brown, with a reddish tinge, too.

After *Captain Blood* and throughout the 'forties, there followed a whole string of films – *The Prince and the Pauper, Robin Hood, Dodge City, They Died With Their Boots On* and *The Adventures of Don Juan* were among the best – on which Warner

Brothers lavished a wealth of talent and money to create fitting vehicles for one who was arguably their brightest star. The pictures were superbly made, and Errol seemed less to act than to *be* the archetypal heroes he played.

He unquestionably improved on his showing in *Captain Blood,* but he remained the natural actor who thought little about technique. His eyes were perhaps his most impressive histrionic equipment, and he used them superbly – making them glint threateningly, for instance, in exciting counterpoint to his speeches to Prince John (Claude Rains) in *Robin Hood.* In the same film and in *The Sea Hawk,* he could talk with rare tenderness and ardour, enough to disarm cynicism, of somewhat nebulous concepts such as freedom and homeland. His intelligent delivery and unaffected sincerity bolstered up a good many banal lines. Reinforced by that erect carriage, his dignity was remarkable and unstudied, never more imposing than in the unforgettable sequence in *The Private Lives of Elizabeth and Essex* in which Elizabeth (Bette Davis) strikes Essex (Flynn) in front of the assembled court and he withdraws through thronged extras the length of an enormous set. The long, graceful promenade comes again in *The Sea Hawk* and *Don Juan.* Or there is his thrilling entry into the banqueting hall in *Robin Hood,* a languid stroll that terminates as he unloads on to a table the carcase of a poached deer that has rested across his shoulders. Errol's sincerity even gave conviction to the military nincompoops featured in *The Charge of the Light Brigade* and *They Died With Their Boots On.*

As early as *Captain Blood,* there were signs that the bravura physical aspects of Flynn's acting were complemented by a less obvious flair for underplaying and gentle, almost tender, humour. Before the camera, his wits never deserted him. If he was frequently defeated by bad dialogue, he never spoiled a good line. The carelessness of his behaviour in *Don Juan* and *The Prince and the Pauper* is in the characters themselves – not in the player.

He was one of the screen's great worriers, closely rivalled, perhaps, only by William Holden. Seldom one for the careless smile or laughing taunt, Errol fought every duel, adding much to their realism, as though he were desperately uneasy about the outcome. And possibly he was. The patent concern of the man crossing swords with Basil Rathbone in *Robin Hood* or Henry Daniell in *The Sea Hawk* might have stemmed from a real fear of accidents. "I don't know much about fencing," he wrote, "but I know how to make it look good." He also knew enough to trust stuntmen and dread the ambitious actor who interpolated, unrehearsed, an extra bit of sword-play that might result in disaster. Whenever he could, Errol worked with doubles for fencing-scenes.

Even in decline and appearing in pictures with little to commend them, he showed flashes of the old flair and panache, so that in the later years he was frequently superior to the films in which he acted.

He was better than he knew, and in the end, in pictures such as *The Sun Also Rises, Too Much, Too Soon,* and *The Roots of Heaven,* he gave the serious performances for which he had craved. His accomplishments were sometimes all the more impressive for being unaided by the screen-plays.

Greatly as his admirers may treasure his last performances, they naturally prefer to think of him as he was at his peak, especially in his romantic adventure movies. They like to hear again that light, clear voice and watch the impeccable bearing that speaks of gallantry, of world-weary casualness, of vanished dreams, of heroic deeds that have no room for brutality, and romance without hint of lust, embellished with wit and style, given substance by noble emotions and honourable intentions. That is the vision of Errol that lingers in the memory, beyond exorcism.

He grew tired of that vision, of course, But there are worse ways of remembering him than as Don Juan with a rapier in one fist and a rose in the other.

Fate has been kind to him. In the two decades following his death, he has lived on in film festivals and in millions of homes around the globe, nightly striving manfully on the smaller screen for those good causes forgotten, if they ever knew them, by the new breed of heroes like James Bond, Harry Palmer and Matt Helm – tired idols and modish bullies whom the cinema Errol would have dispatched with a suave remark and that incomparable style that must remain the envy of all other aspiring swashbucklers.

For Errol, the leap created by *Captain Blood* was enormous. Without moving through the intermediate stages, he had sprung from obscurity to worldwide fame. Suddenly he had wealth and a career, both of which would need careful management. All at once, he was the subject of public adulation and scrutiny. The studio publicity-department, taking their cue from his early life, would colour him with every garish hue that seemed appropriate to the parts they *said* he played in his films. (For example, Errol rarely played a philanderer – whatever he did offscreen.) Like many other superstars, he was not equipped for success on this scale, much as he enjoyed it.

But he coped with that success, it might be argued, as well as most and better than some. If, in the end, he was defeated, he was defeated not by the success itself but by the ease with which it came.

But, then, almost everything came easily to Errol Flynn. He was given – and gave himself – little time to learn.

5

Uncertain Glory

When Errol first met Tiger Lil, as he came to call Lili Damita, she was not only at least five years his senior (her age is hard to verify, but she could have been as much as seven years older than Flynn) but also an established star in both America and Europe, though she was to make few films in the US compared with her husband.

Formerly Lilliane Carré, she had been a dancer at the Folies Bergère, and she was small, her head coming just about up to Errol's shoulder. Her lithe dancer's body must have attracted him instantly, just as he was later to respond to the slim forms of Patrice Wymore and Beverly Aadland, both of them also dancers. But Lili, beautiful as she was, had considerably more status than either of these later partners. Perhaps her greatest successes were already in the past when she met Errol, but she had made *This Is The Night* (1932), *The Match King* (1931) and two important films in 1929 – the part-talkie *The Bridge of San Luis Rey* and (as a sequel to *What Price Glory?*) *The Cockeyed World*, a box-office smash that had been directed by Raoul Walsh, who was also to direct some of her husband's best pictures and become his close friend for a time.

Errol would scarcely have been human if he had not entertained, if only fleetingly, the opportunistic thought that marriage with Lili could do his own career nothing but good. With his rapid success, the juxtaposition was of course inverted, and Lili probably found the experience of being placed in semi-eclipse by her husband little to her taste. In *The Films of Errol Flynn*, a revealing – if also somewhat chilling – anecdote is recounted of Tiger Lil's reaction to Errol's showing in *Captain Blood*. At a party after the première, she was seen to be weeping and imploring some of the guests not to tell Errol how good he was. In so many words, she said that she had lost her husband that night; and she was probably right.

Errol began to enjoy himself – not that he had ever been slow to do that. He wanted to live life to the full, and if his idea of doing so took the form of getting high on booze or dope and chasing girls rather than reading Schopenhauer or listening to Brahms' symphonies, it is not to be wondered at. He was a sensual man, a magnificent animal with a lusty appetite. But he was not totally devoid of a life of the spirit. Not unlike Thoreau, he had written as a young man, "We fritter our lives away in detail", and though with money he did not simplify his existence as he had hoped, at least living deeply, for Errol, was to include finding time to reflect and create through writing. It was this side of him that was so obscured by the other – highly publicized – side of his life, as though there was never any repose in his existence.

There must have been some. Writing is a solitary occupation.

When it came to having a good time, Tiger Lil was no slouch, and Errol asserted that she even taught him a thing or two. He no doubt proved a willing pupil. David Niven's first sight of Lili was at Palm Beach, where she paraded around with a leopard on a leash. She was very lovely, and her idiosyncrasies included having a retinue of homosexual men in respectful attendance. Small wonder, then, that when Niven and Errol first met at her bungalow, they were wary of each other if not actually hostile, though they were later to become friends.

All the evidence indicates that the new marriage began to disintegrate almost before it had begun. The world had always been Errol's oyster. Now it had opened wide for him, and he was not to be tied down by Lili's possessiveness. As well as the fame, he had the money. Even after the returns began to pour in from *Captain Blood,* he said that he was still on $500 a week, but he fought Jack Warner until his salary jumped to four figures a week. Already more than somewhat intoxicated with success, he realized that all strata of society were open to him. Lili hung on tenaciously, but their repeated quarrels and separations garnered bad publicity.

Errol's problem with newspaper reports, then as later, was not getting them but controlling them, attempting to prevent their turning him into a monster. ("Who could live with himself," he once wrote, "believing himself to be a symbol of sex and nothing more?") Warner Brothers tended to be as much taken in by tales of his pre-Hollywood exploits as the most gullible members of the public they sought to manipulate, for there was often that grain of truth, however small, in the stories of his early life. Ironically, the publicity department tried to 'tone down' the more shameful episodes in their new star's career.

Whether he intended to or not, Errol of course fanned the flames by his new life-style. He was a brawler, and he did not exactly avoid trouble, especially in barrooms. But, then, he never had – any more than he had run away from beautiful women. However, the settings were more public now, the names – including his own – more famous. His screen glory was rapidly to find a more lurid public counterpart – notoriety.

During his first year in Hollywood, Errol had become friendly with David Niven. The circumstances of their lives were roughly similar, and they had much in common, though Niven's career was to be a steady progress in the early years, not the accelerating and disorientating snowball that was Flynn's. Accounts are vague about the date, but Errol and he, as Niven has often recalled on television and in his books, shared a bungalow at Santa Monica that they called 'Cirrhosis-by-the-Sea'. (This was in fact one of two guest cottages.within the grounds of Ocean House, the palatial beach-house that William Randolph Hearst had built for Marion Davies. The nickname 'Cirrhosis-by-the-Sea' was provided by Carole Lombard.) The time was presumably before Errol's marriage, but later, probably in 1937 when the drift away from Lili had begun in earnest, the two men once again set up a bachelor-pad at 601 North Linden Drive, Beverly Hills, which they rented from Rosalind Russell. The life-style of these two handsome and carefree actors is not hard to imagine. They had a high old time chasing girls and playing practical jokes on each other. Niven confirms that Errol was smoking or chewing 'kif' ('pot') as he called it in those days. It should be remembered that the substance was not at that time illegal.

With Niven as one of a strong supporting cast, Errol made *The Charge of the Light Brigade* (1936), excitingly well-constructed but fairly mindless entertainment, not helped perhaps by the transposition of the action from the Crimean War of 1853-6 to the India of 1850. Errol's role in this farrago was ludicrously heroic, but he invested the character with a winning sincerity and fierce, if laughable, sense of honour. Once again, he was lucky in his fellow-artists: besides de Havilland in front of the camera and Curtiz behind it, the immensely prolific Max Steiner composed the score, and his superb music did much for the artistic effect of the picture. By this time, though, Errol already had a reputation for ego, and on his next few films he was to be generally disliked by his co-workers, not least for giving little credit for his success to others.

It should be added that the shooting-schedule on *The Charge of the Light Brigade* was possibly the longest and most exacting of Errol's career, the unit suffering the late autumn weather of Lasky Mesa in tents and temporary accommodation.

The hardships suffered by his cast and crew probably did not weigh too heavily upon Michael Curtiz, who had a reputation for driving everybody hard, including himself. More than utterly professional, he was a perfectionist who, from his birth in 1888 to his death in 1962, was to make an estimated 160 films. (Some say at least twenty more.) Born Mihaly Kertesz, he was a Hungarian who began his career inauspiciously, selling sweets in a Budapest theatre, and by his late teens was acting in films – one of which, in 1912, was possibly Hungary's first picture. Curtiz both starred and directed, and by 1925, when he was signed up by Jack Warner, he had made over sixty films in Germany, Austria, France, Sweden and his native-land. Only recently has he become a vogue-director and had the word 'art' applied retrospectively to his enormous output, but during his life-time, nobody ever doubted his complete control and expert manipulation of the material Warners handed him – no matter how unpromising it might have been. He could take a fairly routine project such as *The Breaking Point* and turn it into the best of the several adaptations of Hemingway's *To Have and Have Not.* He was perhaps more interested in editing and camera-movements than in exploiting the subtleties of dialogue, and his linguistic inadequacies produced tales of such malapropisms as: "This will make your blood curl".

As he dominated his material, so Curtiz dominated his actors, and if he had limited concern for their finer feelings, he was certainly not the man to worry overmuch about animals used in *The Charge of the Light Brigade.*

So great was Errol's concern about the treatment of the horses during the making of the film that he complained to the Society for the Prevention of Cruelty to Animals. The way the beasts were handled must have been unusually rough, since Errol confessed later that he himself had been "no angel" with animals during film-making: nobody out to create superior action-sequences could be.

In *My Wicked, Wicked Ways,* he described how horses were made to fall: "A device called 'the running W' was used . . . A trip wire, to make the animals tumble at the right instant. The stunt man, riding the horse, knew where the trip wire was. He knew when he had to get off and all he had to do was take a fall. But the horse would go head-first, and sometimes get hurt and have to be shot. They stopped this because so many horses broke their legs and their necks, and there were protests by the actors and public."

As a result, stunt-riders, for whom Errol had nothing but praise, would train horses so well that they could ride one down the side of a cliff and at a given signal trip the animal by putting a left foot under it. The horse was, so to speak, 'in on the act'.

But pictures like *The Charge of the Light Brigade* took their toll not only of horses. *They Died With Their Boots On* cost Errol a friend, Bill Meade, who was rich, a polo-player, an athlete and an aspirant actor.

A charge against Indians had been run twice over rough terrain in the San Fernando Valley. Meade, with foam on the mouth of his horse, rode next to Errol. The gun went off to signal a third run – with scores and scores of tired men and horses. At the height of the charge, Meade's mount stumbled. The man himself threw away the sword he had been brandishing and prepared to fall. By an unlucky fluke, the weapon landed hilt first and stuck, point upwards. Meade was fatally impaled as he hit the ground in such a way that the blade penetrated heart and lung.

(Even the star was not invulnerable, especially if, as Errol did in the early days, he performed in his own fights. Fencing was particularly dangerous, and best left to professionals, not actors. As Errol put it, "We are Thespians, not fencers." Once, he almost lost an eye to Anthony Quinn's sword, and among miscellaneous hurts he listed repeatedly cut hands and a sword-tip in the mouth.)

By now, Errol had decided that he was in love with Olivia de Havilland, but his way of showing it ("juvenile pranks" was his own description) was not calculated to elicit a favourable reaction, especially since the actress was a mere twenty, while her co-star, even if he was not working at it, was a married man – and inveterate womanizer. The rapport and intimacy that had begun to work so well in their first two films had no real counterpart offscreen.

How sincere were Errol's feelings?

He wrote of them gravely in *My Wicked, Wicked Ways,* but such statements have to be approached with caution, as this book has already made abundantly clear. Nevertheless, there are grounds for believing that his affection was unsimulated and that he was content that his emotions should remain in the realm of romantic longing – chemically pure. Perhaps he had a need for such a love in his life. Olivia de Havilland appears to have represented some sort of ideal for Errol, and Bette Davis writes in her memoirs that he adored her. There is no reason to doubt that they liked each other well enough, but de Havilland evaded him to the end. Possibly Errol wanted it that way, even if only unconsciously.

It is instructive to compare the reputations of Errol Flynn and Olivia de Havilland. There were stars, Errol among them, who seemed to live their lives in public, and the public of the 'thirties, 'forties and later lapped up all the newspaper-stories about them, the more spicy and scandalous the better. Whether he liked publicity or not is in a sense immaterial: Errol's life-style invited it and generated it; he did much of his loving and fighting out in the open.

Ronald Colman, to cite a star of somewhat earlier vintage, was different. He was the perfect gentleman on and off the set, no breath of scandal ever touching him. He had a public existence on the screen, while his private life was his own.

It was in this mould that Olivia de Havilland was cast. Errol called her "a lady", and whatever one might think about that outmoded term, it was accurate. If she was "distant" – a word he also used about her – her remoteness existed mainly in contrast to the impudent, all-too-intimate Flynn. The chemistry that worked potently on the screen not surprisingly lacked the ingredients in real life that might have encouraged Errol to look more hopefully on his infatuation.

After the visual brilliance of *The Charge of the Light Brigade,* his next important picture, preceded by the rather feeble *Green Light,* was *The Prince and the Pauper* (1937). In effect, Errol played a supporting role, but he was dashing in costume again, and his self-effacing performance was delightfully casual, though he had comparatively little to do and was off the screen for lengthy sections of this two-hour picture. Even so, his scenes with the twin boys Billy and Bobby Mauch have real charm and suggest a genuine feeling for children, as well as a considerable sense of humour.

Surprisingly, when one considers their later partnership on and off the screen, Alan Hale appears in *The Prince and the Pauper* as an enemy of Errol and is dispatched during some fairly routine swordplay.

It must have been obvious to Errol at this stage that fencing was going to be important to his career, but characteristically the man who looked a better dancer than he actually was did little to improve his skill with a blade except rely on his natural athleticism. He could handle his fists well up to a point, though he was to work hard to portray *Gentleman Jim* (1942). He was an excellent swimmer and tennis-player. There are conflicting stories about his horsemanship, but what one sees on the screen alone gives the lie to the absurd notion that he could not sit a saddle. However, he lacked the interest and application to practise fencing. Why attempt to do in fact what he *looked* as though he was doing with consummate ease?

The attitude could be contrasted with that of another actor, Basil Rathbone, who took many lessons from the master, Fred Cavens, and who, if he is remembered for nothing else, will be recalled for his thrilling swordplay against Errol in *Robin Hood* and his climactic fight with Tyrone Power in *The Mark of Zorro.*

The difference between the two actors tells us something about Rathbone and a great deal about Errol.

The next Flynn pictures were *Another Dawn,* largely forgotten except for a lovely melody by Erich Wolfgang Korngold, and *The Perfect Specimen,* Errol's first comedy. This side of him the public never encouraged Warner Brothers to develop – a pity, because his flair was apparent and he might well have emerged as another Cary Grant or, if his friend's later parts are recalled, David Niven. The light touch was authentically there, though it had to find expression in Errol's adventure movies. One of his biggest differences of opinion with Jack Warner concerned the studio-boss's inflexible view of his star – always, of course, based on the concept of commercial movie-making.

Probably the earliest clash between the two came about through Errol's collapse on-set during the shooting of *Captain Blood.* The star had been hit by a bout of malaria, but he finished the scene after downing a bottle of cognac. (So Errol wrote; if the account was true, the wonder was that he was not killed by the cure.) The next day, he received a blue note – the colour denoted the worst of bad news: a kind of Jack Warner code – asking him to see Mr Warner. An inside tip told Errol that the rushes of the previous day's work had shown a drunken actor bawling lines that were not in the script.

Meeting trouble in advance, he made up his mind to tell the big boss exactly where to go, but when the opportunity actually came, he did nothing to defend himself, he confessed, merely promising that there would be no more "Flynn-anigans".

Later encounters were not to be so bland.

Perhaps Jack Warner, very much the self-made man, saw things with a perspective unknown to Errol, who had achieved what he had achieved early and with accelerating ease. Warner had come up the hard way. At the age of eleven, he had sung as a soprano between reels in Ohio, where he and his brothers had toured showing films. Something of a philistine ("I would rather take a fifty-mile hike than crawl through a book"), he was also an autocrat, a fighter and a stayer. He and his brothers Harry and Albert resisted and survived many stockholders' attempts to oust them, and in the 'sixties, after Errol's death, Jack Warner, then over seventy, personally supervised the production of *My Fair Lady* and *Camelot.* This tough, feisty little man might well have admired, especially at first, his new star's impudence and spirit. But there were limits – and he made them clear. Studio-bosses ran true to type, and always *they* ruled – not the stars they employed. Errol was to learn that the fight against Jack Warner, though minor battles could be won from him, was a one-sided affair. Warner, who invariably gave the public what it wanted, knew to the last dollar in what roles that public liked Errol Flynn best, and he was determined that the actor should stay within this highly profitable range.

Even so, they maintained a somewhat strange comradeship, partly because Jack Warner was a divided personality: outside the office, according to Errol, he could rival his star in charm; but at work he was ruthlessly the businessman. Eventually, Errol conquered his fear of the second to the extent of stretching out his feet in Warner's office, once kicking off his shoes in a calculated gesture of imperturbability.

In 1938 Errol made *The Adventures of Robin Hood,* the film for which he is perhaps best remembered. *Photoplay* called it "magnificent entertainment", but that is an understatement. Of *Robin Hood,* Frank Nugent, later to write such John Ford movies as *Fort Apache* and *She Wore a Yellow Ribbon,* said in *The New York Times* of 13th May 1938: "A richly produced, bravely bedecked, romantic and colourful show, it leaps boldly to the front of this year's best and can be calculated to rejoice the eights, rejuvenate the eighties and delight those in between." His words sum up the universal appeal of Flynn's most popular film. Its brilliance shows in all aspects, and it has stylistic bravura and panache that have rarely been captured in any other production. Time has dulled neither its élan nor the beautiful Technicolor tints of a process that is no longer used. The screenplay is elegant and pointed, the plot tight and the characters straightforward without being insipid. Errol and de Havilland played some of their most affecting love-scenes in a relationship that was all the better for being seen to progress and change with the action. Rathbone made a superb villain, finally subdued only after a thrilling duel, staged by Fred Cavens, that took the antagonists all over Nottingham Castle. Korngold's sumptuous score was one of the finest of his Hollywood career, subtly wedded to the action, and Sol Polito and Tony Gaudio produced unforgettable images with the camera.

William Keighley began shooting in late 1937, but he was replaced by Curtiz, perhaps because of the latter's reputation as a director of action and to impose greater style on the material. The budget was eventually inflated to $2 million – Warners' greatest up to that time.

As for Errol, his performance was splendid – heroic, chivalrous, athletic and humorous. He wore tights, soft leather boots and jerkins tied with string as though he had been born in them, and his Robin Hood possessed the natural authority to control such lively merry men as Alan Hale and Eugene Pallette. Errol's light voice comes ringing down the years as one recalls Robin's "I've called you here as free-born Englishmen" when the Saxons have assembled in the forest to hear his plans, or his "Welcome to Sherwood, my Lady" to Marion (de Havilland) after Sir Guy of Gisbourne (Rathbone) and his retinue have been trapped in one of the most amusing and exhilarating ambushes ever screened.

Errol noted in his autobiography that he did all his own stunts in *Robin Hood,* and he had cause for pride. They also satisfied a psychological need: he had reached a stage at which he needed to demonstrate his bravery, if only to himself.

In *My Wicked, Wicked Ways,* Errol has left us his own impression of his movie-making in the 'thirties: "You went from one picture to another swiftly, a month or two or three for the making of each. There'd be a half-dozen pictures 'in the can' and you'd be making your sixth or seventh, with the others not yet released. Then they released them, one after another, every month or two, and you found yourself a household word, famous all over the movie-going sphere."

There is no indication at all that he realized how important these pictures would be, that their qualities would endure forty years later, that they would grant him at least twenty years of fame after his death – and perhaps even immortality. The very nature of the historical romances has helped to preserve their freshness, since Errol's costume-roles have a timelessness that makes it difficult to realize that *Robin Hood,* say, is nearly forty years old.

In some ways, Errol was an intellectual snob – like those critics who find masterpieces only among masterpieces or, in Cyrano's words, "true genius only among Geniuses". Their star did not truly realize the excellence of *Captain Blood, The Charge of the Light Brigade, The Prince and the Pauper* and, latest, *Robin Hood.* His autobiography contains the amazing sentence: "I developed a disgust for the mediocre vehicles to which I was assigned." More realistically, he feared becoming typecast and longed to grow in a variety of parts. Earlier, his agent had told him that MGM were to make *Romeo and Juliet,* and though he made some effort to play Romeo (on the screen, that was), he failed, the role going to Leslie Howard.

Except in terms of box-office grosses, film-stars are rarely good judges of their own work, and Errol was not alone in underestimating the Warner Brothers productions. Olivia de Havilland also strove for what she hoped would be better parts in better pictures. Years later, there were public utterances indicating her realization that these *were* the better pictures.

However, in fairness to both Errol and Olivia de Havilland,

it must be admitted that their films together, superb though they were, made modest demands of them as actors. She was to achieve more in such pictures as *The Snake Pit* and *The Heiress,* and Errol had a long wait before *The Sun Also Rises* and *The Roots of Heaven.* The paradox is that perhaps only *The Heiress,* of the four pictures just cited, presented such *overall* accomplishment as the Warner Brothers films in which Flynn and de Havilland co-starred.

Besides discontent over his work, justified or not, other pressures were being exerted on Errol. They ranged from the weekly thousands of fan-letters to the fights with Lili that were not private but received almost daily exposure in the press. Her possessiveness was strangling him, he said, though in virtually the same breath he admitted that it did not inhibit his pursuit of beautiful women. (Words like "chase" and "pursue" in this context are misleading, it might be argued: there is meagre evidence that many of them ran away.)

There was some diversion and relief from domestic strife when, early in 1937, his old pal Koets surfaced in Hollywood and they took off for the war in Spain.

According to Errol, while they were at the Gran Via Hotel in Madrid, one morning at nine shells ripped through the building opposite, taking off one corner. He and Koets ran down to the lobby, where an unperturbed clerk said, "That's the Germans. They always shell at nine o'clock."

Among other adventures was an episode during which Koets tried to become familiar with a girl-partisan who whipped out a gun from between her breasts and rammed it into his belly. When this gesture failed to damp his ardour, the girl fired, and the bullet, passing through Koet's shirt, creased his skin.

They were in Algeciras at the time. Errol had been commissioned by William Randolph Hearst to cable stories, though he had yet to send a dispatch. (What 'stories' Hearst wanted is uncertain, but the anecdotes Errol later told were vivid enough.) He was pondering Koet's near-lethal dalliance when a shell exploded and the balcony beneath which Errol was standing collapsed. He went out like a light and woke up in hospital, where he recovered a few days later.

One result was that headlines screamed in the press: "Errol Flynn killed in Spain".

That much at least is true. But the most tolerant reader of *My Wicked, Wicked Ways* would merely shrug over the rest, including the obligatory torrid romance with a Spanish miss.

In the same year, Errol also published *Beam Ends,* the account of his seven-month voyage in 1930 from Sydney to New Guinea.

Already the star was tired of speaking other men's words, personifying other men's heroic visions and doing the artistic bidding of those who occasionally cared little for his own ideas – the directors.

But that was not his reason for writing *Beam Ends.* Its date of publication makes it clear that the book had been composed *before* the growing dissatisfaction with acting – essentially an interpretive art.

Good or bad, *Beam Ends* stemmed from a clear literary urge of long standing.

Of Errol's three books, it is arguably the most successful taken as a whole. Both *Showdown* and the autobiography are wildly unequal, but this first attempt at sustained literary achievement tends – or at least tries – to disarm criticism. However, it is not entirely successful. Despite the attempt to invest the goings-on ashore and afloat with some allure or appealing innocence, the reader may well be left with the impression that Errol and his friends were a wild, rowdy bunch – their antics not completely to be excused by youth.

Overall, the style is anecdotal, and the attendant facetiousness can become trying. Knowing well his own charm, the author probably miscalculated: such a quality may be easy to radiate in person, but it is much harder to inject it into cold print. The twinkle in the Flynn eye defied translation into his own books. Errol was never to find a literary equivalent; he simply never developed his gift to the point at which he might have accomplished the feat.

Still, though frequently ungrammatical, the language is refreshingly simple and unpretentious, approaching the uncomfortably 'literary' only in some of the longer passages of

Errol, Theodore and Marelle Flynn visit Catalina Island, Los Angeles, 1939

The charmer fails to charm: Errol and two indifferent canine friends

Dodge City: Errol, Olivia de Havilland and Ann Sheridan

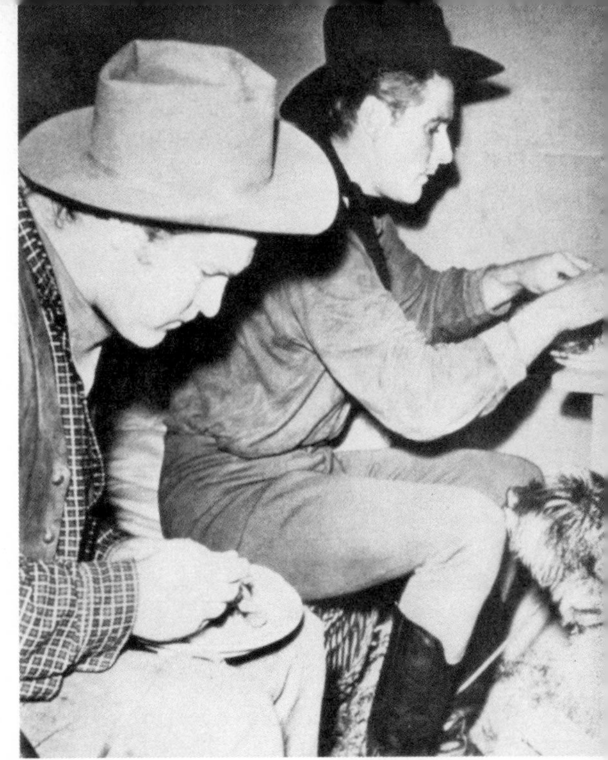

Virginia City: Errol and Guinn ('Big Boy') Williams (with Arno) share a lunch-break

Errol takes a shower after tennis

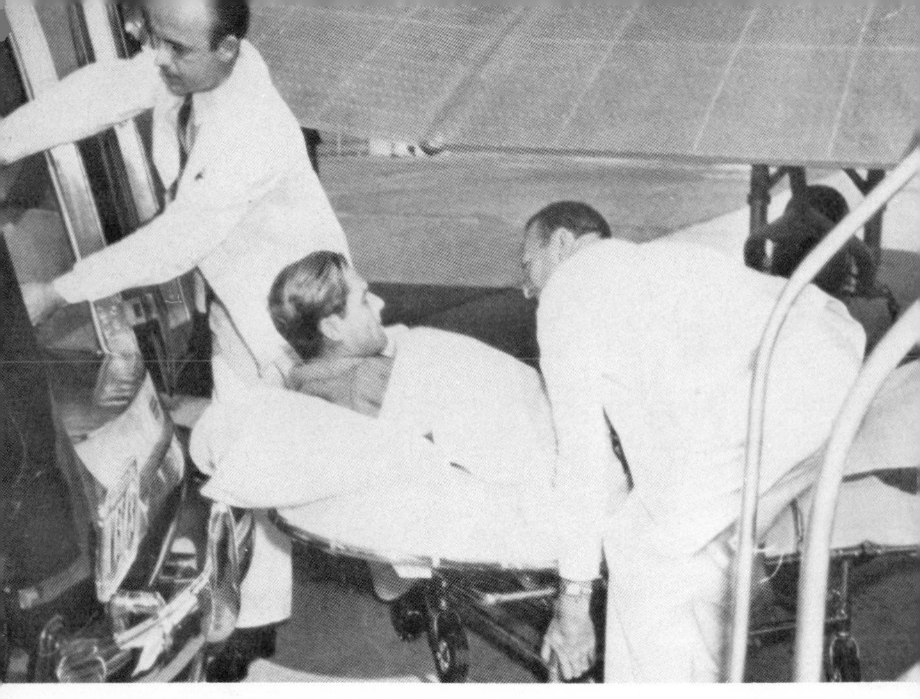

Flat out – with influenza – leaving plane after trip to South America

Errol with Claude Rains on the set of *The Sea Hawk*

Michael Curtiz (director) and Errol look serious about a scene from *Virginia City*

The dreadful effects of eating onions: Errol and Olivia de Havilland in a scene from *They Died With Their Boots On*

At the rape trial: a tight spot, but Errol looks unimpressed

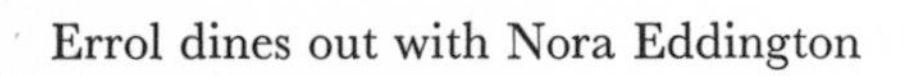

Errol dines out with Nora Eddington

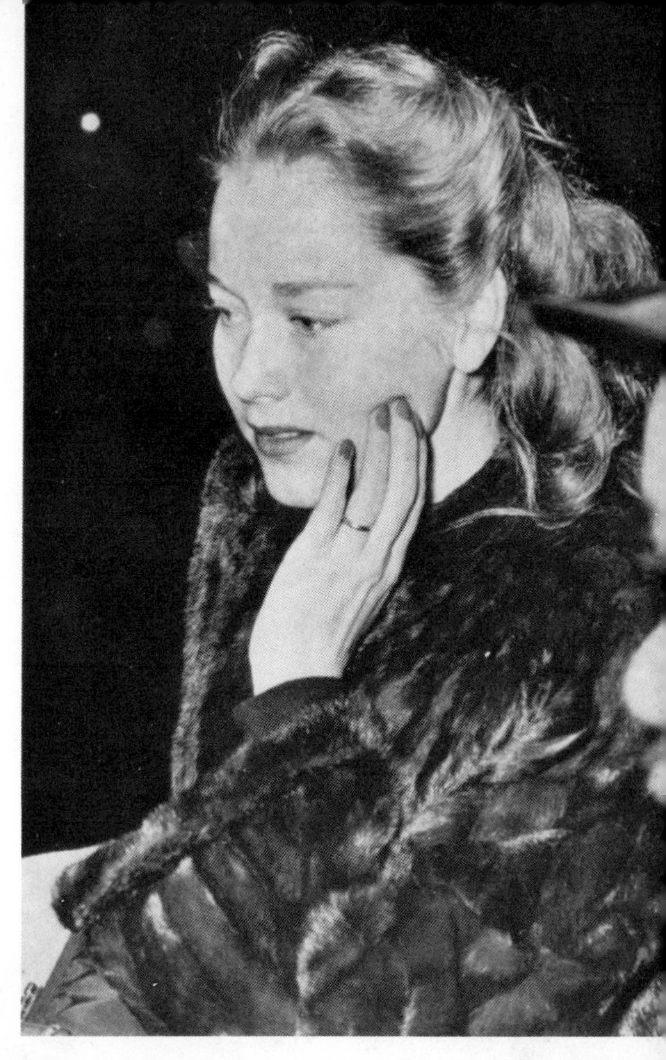

Nora returns from Mexico City after the birth of Deirdre

Errol with band-leader Xavier Cugat at the opening of Ciro's

Errol and Arno on board the *Zaca*

description or the gusty eloquence with which Errol delivers his Deep Thoughts on sailing:

"Man against the sea! An old story, but who has been faced with its perils and not known his weakness? Or felt that utter helplessness and despair against its fury?"

Such drama and rhetoric had a Victorian quality that one would have thought wholly out of place in the mid-'thirties – whether the author had yet become steeped in the American vernacular or not.

Elsewhere, Errol can wax jocularly – and clumsily – verbose, as in a passage describing how Johnson, the pugilistic journalist of Rockhampton, is struck by a flying saltcellar at a party:

"Subconsciously we come to formulate fixed ideas of the reactions of our acquaintances to certain circumstances. Their failure to behave in the manner expected causes a shock of surprise. A metal saltcellar, suddenly and violently impinging on the forehead for no apparent reason, is apt to inspire resentment in the mildest individual, particularly when it provokes a burst of girlish mirth at his expense."

As if not quite confident of the intrinsic interest of the voyage, Errol makes sure of having a generous quota of Colourful Characters to excite chuckles and astonishment. Goodyear, their host at Tavia, is a notable example.

At the beginning of a meal served by native girls wearing only grass skirts, Goodyear, according to Errol, dropped his false teeth in a glass of water. On the table, he had a long nasty-looking pistol with which he later interrupted the meal to take a potshot at a native lurking outside. When Errol suggested these methods might be somewhat extreme, he explained loftily, "Oh, it doesn't hurt 'em much. These air pistols don't do much damage, you know. If I didn't have this," he patted the weapon affectionately, "they'd steal every damn thing I've got in my store. I always aim for the arse – if I score a bull's-eye, I win a cigar. Ha, ha. Then all they've got to do is go back to their village and dig the slug out."

(This was a travesty of a real character, who, after the publication of *Beam Ends,* would no doubt have shot its author if he could have got him in his sights.)

The Colourful Characters, aided by artistic licence, dutifully go through their paces, but Errol can sometimes be accused of playing his vivid tales for more than they are worth.

There are generous measures of adventure, long passages of nautical observations and many descriptions, often nicely managed, of flora and fauna. Reflections on Life are kept to a minimum, and perhaps that is also an asset. Essentially picaresque, the narrative, if one separates it from the literary travelogue, fails to present the sailors as quite the engaging quartet Errol doubtless hoped to depict. The reader might be forgiven for seeing them as carousing louts, a danger to themselves and to others, rather than as four stylish young men on an inquiring – if not spiritual – odyssey.

At the end, nothing has changed (if we overlook Trelawny's 'death'), nothing has been learned – perhaps not even better seamanship, since Errol was to stick the *Sirocco* on a reef soon after the voyage was over.

All this said, he managed to recapture a modicum of the feeling of that early fling, the irresponsible craziness that characterizes the brief immortality of youth. Looking back at the escapades some five years later, he had perhaps learned something at least, because he wrote in the Foreword:

"Doubtless there is a providence, some special planetary influence for the express purpose of protecting youth from the consequences of its own folly."

6

Too Much, Too Soon

In 1938, though neither film was quite outstanding of its type, *Four's a Crowd* (whacky comedy) and *The Sisters* (domestic drama) gave Errol some of the variety he claimed he was missing, and he did notably well – in the first as a public-relations consultant and in the second as a failure with a weakness for drink. In the same year, *Dawn Patrol,* directed by Edmund Goulding, found Flynn and Niven together again (to say nothing of Flynn and Rathbone) in a World War I story of aviation – a remake of Howard Hawks' earlier version. The picture was a satisfying achievement, with an innocence about its heroics that was hard to resist, a genuine feeling of comradeship among the fliers and a stoicism that was quietly moving. All three principals performed admirably, and the rapport between Flynn and Niven, especially in their more lighthearted scenes, was obvious.

Working on the picture, Niven observed that Errol had become quite a prima donna.

Stars often are. Or are frequently said to be. Even by those who disclaim their own part in an unnatural concentration of focus, they are scrutinized too closely. Sometimes, if a star's conduct is acceptable to begin with, it breaks down under that merciless attention. Humphrey Bogart once remarked: "I have politeness and manners. I was brought up that way. But in this goldfish-bowl life, it is sometimes hard to use them."

Though unattractive, Errol's behaviour was scarcely surprising. In his late twenties, with a hectic life behind him as dubious preparation, he had been swept up by fame and success. Even with Errol's predilections, the story might have been different if the process had been more gradual and not on such an overwhelming scale. As it was, he was not coping too well with the obligations of being a star but enjoying himself immensely as the man of the moment. He was coming to terms with marriage mainly by acting like a bachelor, and if he had hoped for self-discipline and stability in his union with Lili, he must soon have forgotten that aspiration. With money, his life seemed to change not in quality, as he had hoped, but merely in quantity – more booze, more girls, more possessions. The new dimensions of his existence were predictable and sadly stereotyped. For a man who had earlier talked in terms, however vague, of a spiritual odyssey ("I am going to front the essentials of life to see if I can learn what it has to teach . . . "), there was not much sense of progress, and he showed no signs of tiring of philandering or needing more nourishment from a woman than that provided by amorous one-night stands.

In his *New Guinea Notebook* (1933), Errol penned aphorisms like these:

"The best part of life is spent earning money in order to enjoy a questionable liberty during the least valuable part of it. To hell with money. Pursuit of it is not going to mould my life for me

"I am going to live sturdily and spartan-like – to drive life into a corner and reduce it to its lowest terms and if I find it sublime I shall know it by experience – and not make wistful conjectures about it conjured up by illustrated magazines. I refuse to accept the ideology of a business world which believes that man at hard work is the noblest work of God . . .

"To learn what is worth one's while is the largest part of the art of life. Just one hour of life is far more important than money, for time is life.

"Whenever you waste your time over printed words that neither enlighten nor amuse you, you are, in a sense, committing suicide. The value, the intrinsic value, of our actions, emotions, thoughts, possessions, occupations, the manner in which we are living – this is the first thing to be determined, for unless we are satisfied that any of these things has a true value, our lives are futile and there is no more hopeless realization than this."

The way in which Errol was living sowed the seeds of his later destruction – or, if that assertion borders on the melodramatic, at least laid the ground for big trouble that was not too far over the horizon. He was already shaping up as a natural target for moralists. His tastes were intensifying towards the point at which he could no longer modify them even if he wanted to – in short, addiction. Had he stopped to think, he already knew that even in Hollywood respectability counted. In his autobiography, he commented that after their marriage those who had shunned him and Lili for merely living together came calling. Yet he continued, almost compulsively, to provoke and outrage morality.

Did he care?

Well, he was to be made to care.

"My only real happiness is when I am near the sea," he wrote, and after a reconciliation with Lili and the improvement of his contract with Warner Brothers, he bought a sailboat that he named the *Sirocco* after the earlier craft he had owned in New Guinea. Using the name again was bad luck, he seemed to have decided later, not surprisingly. No guests on board were asked their ages, and the oversight was to have serious consequences.

He hoped to interest Lili in the sea, to share his great love with her, and they set sail for the islands of the West Indies. However enjoyable the seafaring, domestic life was not smooth-sailing, and in Havana Errol broke loose for a typical picaresque adventure during which he was besieged in a whorehouse by a mob of his fans. The episode had an almost symbolic or surrealistic force, though Errol appeared to be unaware of it.

He recharged his physical batteries, but claimed that his nerves were in bad shape. *Life* photographers caught up with him in Miami, and later he found himself in swimtrunks on the cover of the magazine on 23rd May 1938. The caption read: "ERROL FLYNN, Glamour Boy". "There I was," Errol commented, "looking eager, young, happy, posed with my chin on my fist, wearing a thin line of moustache, and looking gaily at the world – on top of which, supposedly, I was sitting."

It *was* the period when he had, in the words of David Niven, "endless fun". One of Errol's characteristic anecdotes was about his habit of buying animals when he was drunk. During one such impulsive spree, he purchased a female lion-cub, which he unloaded at a hotel in Chicago, saying that Mrs Flynn would call for it later.

But amidst all this frivolity, he noticed a significant change in his sex-life, for having been the pursuer, he now increasingly tended to become the pursued. Hunter and prey had swapped places, and those who tracked him down were not all stars like Lupe Velez, the so-called 'Mexican spitfire', with whom, according to him, Errol had at least one wild night; the predatory females included many who, as unknowns, sought to get ahead in the rat-race of Hollywood, so that Errol, as a prelude to lovemaking, would warn them that they had no chance of obtaining a part in his next picture.

A psychologist once told Errol: "One of the reasons for the public interest in you as a personality is that there is a certain amount of general male identification with the life you lead. Many men would like to be living as you are doing." Like so many of the comments on Errol, it was an oversimplification. In a special sense, Flynn was a surrogate figure: he had the mistresses whom most men dreamed about but would also have run a mile to escape in real life.

One of the social groups to which he belonged was the Olympiads, an association whose exclusiveness was based on a man's claim to be unique rather than on his riches or fame. Nevertheless, membership included some household names – among them John Barrymore; Gene Fowler, the author who was later to write Barrymore's biography, *Good Night, Sweet Prince;* John Decker, the artist and central figure of the club; and, as well as other actors, Alan Mowbray and W. C. Fields. The Olympiads appears to have been mainly a talking-club, usually meeting at Decker's house, but the uncharitable might observe that the membership was largely made up of some formidable drinkers. Errol did more listening then talking, though he would occasionally regale the others with tales of New Guinea.

How many facts he got right is anybody's guess.

There was a subsidiary group scatologically called the Oh, Shit Club. In his autobiography, Errol explained the rules.

All bores were allowed to corner their victims and speak for two and a half minutes, at the end of which time the victim had to look the bore straight in the eye, murmur a deflating "Oh, shit!" and walk away. If you were caught lowering your eyes or turning away prematurely, you were expelled from the Oh, Shit Club.

Meanwhile, Errol's fights with Jack Warner about improved contracts and better parts were continuing. Errol would tell himself that if the worst came to the worst, he could always quit motion pictures and return to his former life. How serious he was is open to question.

Many are the reasons that have been given for enjoying the life of a Hollywood celebrity, including Robert Mitchum's "It beats working" and Harry Cohn's "It beats pimping". But Errol would have had to admit that a star's life, whatever its difficulties, beat any sort of existence he had led or conceivably could lead in Australia or New Guinea, even with the capital he then possessed.

In any case, moving on was his speciality – not going back. There were unpaid bills, stolen jewels, cuckolded husbands and old enemies in his past life – not to mention all the folk who would undoubtedly greet him as a phoney and a poseur. Besides, he had known the fleshpots, the high life and the heady wine of adulation, and his appetites were still strong.

Did a hungry man walk away from a banquet?

David Niven went off to war in 1939, but Errol continued to make films. In *My Wicked, Wicked Ways,* the man who penned uninhibited revelations about so much of his private life is strangely reticent about his remaining a civilian after the outbreak of hostilities. His silence might well be interpreted as a painful sensitivity. His failure to join up has certainly been vilified and mocked, both at the time and as recently as the 'sixties – long after the facts should have been known. But his status as a civilian did him little real harm with his public, even GI's envying him for his women, his career and his remaining stateside.

What it did to Errol was another matter.

The truth was that his health disqualified him from service.

(In 1942 he became a naturalized American, but that small detail did not prevent his being scorned in some quarters as an *Australian* who was taking refuge from conscription in the US.) The tennis-star and super-athlete had a heart-murmur and was to be rejected by every branch of the armed services. Once again, appearances were deceptive: the perfect specimen still *looked* perfect, but besides the cardiac condition, there were hints of other disorders, among them tuberculosis and recurrent malaria. What drink and drugs had also wrought by this time is conjectural, but Errol had already sampled opium according to his own account, and his pleasures drove him hard.

He did not advertise the fact that his draft-rating was 4F. However, it seems certain that his physical condition caused him no little distress. To start with, he was still a relatively young man. Then there was the disparity between his screen-identity and the real person: the heroic Flynn of picture after picture could not join in the authentic heroics of a world war. His greatest contribution to the war-effort was to be films such as *Desperate Journey, Edge of Darkness* and *Objective, Burma!,* though he was to be bitterly hurt by the reception of the last.

Just as he had suffered in silence the psychological problems of his marriage, he stoically kept to himself the complicated feelings engendered by his exclusion from the fighting.

He made *Dodge City,* his first Western and a masterly piece of work, its ingredients confidently welded together by Michael Curtiz. They included a rather weak screenplay that was compensated by other strengths such as one of Max Steiner's most sumptuous scores. With little to do, Olivia de Havilland was charming, and she and Flynn played well yet again. The list of players included several members of the Flynn 'clan': Bruce Cabot, Alan Hale and Guinn 'Big Boy' Williams – "not so much a cast as a brewery" (to borrow Robert Mitchum's words about another picture).

The cast also contained the 'Oomph Girl', Ann Sheridan, and it was a pity that, dramatically, her path and Errol's scarcely crossed. Her unrefined but unmistakable honesty might have combined well with his polish, and their scenes together in the later *Edge of Darkness* had a special warmth, though the picture devoted comparatively little time to their relationship. In a third film, *Thank Your Lucky Stars,* they never met in any real sense, each working in separate segments of an all-star extravaganza. As true co-stars they were to work together once more, on *Silver River* in 1948, but though Errol gave a much better performance than the film deserved, the screenplay lacked coherence, so that his cinematic relationship with Ann Sheridan was marred by inadequate dialogue.

Dodge City has at least one sequence that vividly illustrates the thesis that the screen Errol was a good deal more responsible than the delight of the gossip-columnists. The feckless Alan Hale, Flynn's side-kick, having promised to behave himself, drifts into a ladies' temperance meeting, where he expounds on his former boozy ways. (This must have been something of an esoteric joke.) Suddenly, a brawl erupts in the saloon next door, and with a whoop of relief and joy, Hale finds himself engulfed by one of the largest-scale fights ever filmed, in which the entire saloon is virtually demolished. When the dust settles, Cabot and his baddies decide that someone must pay and seize upon Hale for a lynching, from which he is rescued only by the intervention of Errol, who had warned him against the dangers in the first place.

The situation – mature hero shepherding irresponsible old-timer – is archetypal in Flynn films. Errol saved his own rashness and stupidity for offscreen.

Warner Brothers overcame the problem of starring an Englishman (or an English-*sounding* man) in a Western by giving to the character played by Errol a pedigree that included Irish origins and many years of globe-trotting, but audiences, loving every minute of the film, were not concerned about such sophistries. Warners never 'explained' their star's accent again, though his autobiography would have it differently. According to Errol (he was wrong), there were two lines in all his Westerns that ran as follows:

HEAVY: Where you from, pardner?
FLYNN: I happen to come from Ireland, but I am as American as you are.

While he confessed that they were undoubtedly successful, Errol also asserted that he was embarrassed by his Westerns, believing he was ridiculously miscast. Furthermore, they did nothing for his desire to play real characters – "to get swords and horses to hell out of [his] life".

In the same year – 1939 – as *Dodge City,* he made *The Private Lives of Elizabeth and Essex,* again with Curtiz in charge. Though the trappings were good – fine sets and costumes, a distinguished Korngold score, impressive playing from Davis as Elizabeth – the film did not display one of Errol's better performances, and his inadequacy as Essex might have been a reflection of his general unhappiness about the production. The adaptation from Maxwell Anderson's stolid play was heavy going, and Errol probably knew it, since he handled his lines with little care. More than that, studio-politics surrounding the picture must have made him uneasy.

Queen not only in the picture but also of the Warner Brothers lot, Bette Davis was then earning about $5,000 a week while Errol was on six. Temperamentally, the two leading players were worlds apart, and though Davis was easily the more professional actor, Errol was among the biggest box-office attractions in the country. There was trouble about the title of the film (was it to be *Essex and Elizabeth* or *Elizabeth and Essex*?) and disappointment over the casting: Davis had wanted Olivier to play opposite her. Shooting thus began in an atmosphere not conducive to rapport, and according to Errol, when Bette Davis, called upon to strike Essex, actually hit Errol with stunning force during a rehearsal, he went back to his dressing-room and threw up. (This could well be true, certainly as an illustration of his sensitivity. Here was a man who could be cut to the quick by a bad notice, particularly a few years later in his career when performances that he considered 'straight' and at least adequate were panned by New York critics.) After Errol had remonstrated privately with his co-star, the actress said that she could not do the scene any other way. However, when the cameras rolled, she threw a perfect stage-slap that looked good but did not connect. Errol stated that this improvement was the result of her having inspected the homicide in his eyes. By his account, there was a sequel in which he, as Essex, playfully slapped the Queen's bottom during a rehearsal, using some of the force Davis had exerted on him. Her reaction was predictable, and Errol said, "I'm awfully sorry. I don't know how to do it any other way".

He had taken top billing over her in *The Sisters,* but the two were never to act together again.

Bette Davis has since in interviews denied that there was friction between them, though she admitted that Errol, not understanding the impulses of one who wished to perfect her craft, asked her repeatedly why she worked so hard. To him, acting was a game.

Perhaps so. He scarcely impressed anyone, then or later, as a dedicated actor or one eager to learn. But though he talked of "walking through" his parts, he performed more than adequately in his most famous roles, bestowing unique distinction upon them. For this insecure, sensitive man, who longed for more demanding work, there was a form of insurance in being the first to categorize Flynn as a lousy actor, one to whom it was all a game. The inconsistencies in his attitude to his art are not hard to spot.

Bette Davis's professed liking for Errol must be balanced against reports that David O. Selznick's notion of borrowing Flynn and Davis to play Scarlett O'Hara and Rhett Butler in *Gone with the Wind* was vetoed by Miss Davis, who found appalling the idea of Errol as Butler.

Errol made two more Westerns close together – *Virginia City* and *Santa Fe Trail* (1940). In the first, he turned in a sound performance that triumphed over indifferent material, and the second was noteworthy for extraneous reasons. A Warners publicity-junket took place in Santa Fe, New Mexico, to boost the picture. The studio set three men working twenty-four hours a day to keep Errol sober and out of trouble. They failed.

Between the Westerns, he starred in *The Sea Hawk,* one of the best films he was ever to make. Curtiz directed with great virtuosity; Errol looked perfect and handled elegant dialogue with consummate ease; Korngold again set musical standards that have never been surpassed. At one time, Technicolor and

Olivia de Havilland had been considered, but eventually Brenda Marshall played the female lead, and Sol Polito's photography was in black and white. Henry Daniell made a villain every inch and sneer as polished as Rathbone, and his duel with Flynn in the closing sequence is a model for a clash with rapiers. As usual, Fred Cavens staged the fight, though both actors were doubled whenever possible.

Once again, through its all-round excellence, a Flynn picture highlighted the complicated nature of Errol's complaints about his roles. The point might be granted that they made limited demands of him; but they fitted perfectly into a satisfying artistic whole – at least in the best examples.

Errol undervalued his best films. Failing to appreciate his own accomplishments as an actor, he was too ready to dismiss such inestimable feats as conveying heroism together with a sense of humour, authentic courtliness with unmistakable masculinity. Not entirely incorrectly, he suspected that he was being admired for his thighs. His failure to appreciate the Warner vehicles as fine films stemmed directly from an unawareness that in the creative world trash (not that films like *Robin Hood* were trash) has an unnerving habit of turning into art and art (perhaps not excluding *Elizabeth and Essex*) into trash.

Nor did he ever face the responsibility of his aspirations. If he wanted roles of greater subtlety and depth, he had, like Olivia de Havilland, to jeopardize an established career as a star in order to appear in different pictures – and not necessarily better ones. As Errol was to find out, nobody could guarantee that more three-dimensionally conceived characters would inevitably occur within the context of good films; and when he played Mike Campbell, for example, in *The Sun Also Rises,* the picture proved to be leaden and unequal. At the height of his career as a swashbuckler, he could no doubt have had for the asking stage-parts that would have required a greater range of acting. But that course, too, would have meant turning his back, however temporarily, on the business of being a star.

Errol Flynn had neither the strength nor the desire to do so. (Since his arrival in Hollywood, he had made seventeen pictures. In a mere six years or less, Warner Brothers had made him an enormous financial and popular success, and by the time he was involved in the fiasco of his own production of *William Tell* in the early 'fifties, it was estimated that he had made approximately eight million dollars, mainly from appearing in Warner Brothers pictures. He was willing enough to accept big money, and he could not with justice blame Warners for putting him in profitable vehicles that justified his salary.)

One other ingredient in his career gave him genuine, if considerably less obvious, cause for grievance. The nobility of most of his parts, so much at variance with his own nature, was increasingly difficult to live with. It is an actor's job to play at being somebody he is not; but audience-response and publicity had combined to superimpose his heroic screen-image powerfully on Errol the man – and it hurt and worried him.

In the following year, 1941, he made two fairly routine pictures, *Footsteps in the Dark* and *Dive Bomber,* both in modern dress, but he returned West and to costume for *They Died With Their Boots On* (1942), in which, as George Armstrong Custer, Errol was shown in a full range of the moods for which he was so popular. Though there was no depth to the screenplay, neither humour nor pathos was neglected, but they did not slow the pace of the film or detract from impressive action-sequences. For once, the character Errol played, if he had his noble side, also revealed some of the impudent rascality and insubordination that were in Flynn himself. Both star and screenwriters worked hard to make the hero a good deal more sympathetic, though less complicated, than Custer probably was in fact.

They Died With Their Boots On marked a double parting of the ways. Errol had by this time fallen out with Michael Curtiz, and the picture, originally scheduled for direction by him, was handed over to Flynn's friend Raoul Walsh, who had the experience and flair to do a fine job. The film was also notable because Olivia de Havilland, as she and Errol both probably realized, was appearing opposite him for the last time.

She had made plain her resolve to move on to more demanding roles in strongly different pictures, and she made good her vow, though at first progress was not spectacular – hampered somewhat by Warner Brothers' claim for an extra six months on her contract for periods when she had been on suspension. But in 1946 she won a best actress Academy Award for her performance in *To Each His Own,* and three years later she repeated the feat with *The Heiress,* for which she also won the New York Critics' award, as she had done a year earlier for *The Snake Pit.*

Errol Flynn was never to win an Academy Award, but he did, in the end, play a few of the serious parts he had craved. As for the New York critics, his opinion of those gentlemen was no doubt unprintable.

Desperate Journey, a picture of conventional wartime derring-do, and *Gentleman Jim* filled in most of 1942 for Errol at Warners, the second being one of his favourite films. It certainly did more than employ his skills as a boxer. Between the star and the historical James J. Corbett, there were more than superficial resemblances, and Errol was happy, for all the unequal nature of the script, playing a cocky, charming and irrepressible adventurer who was not too far removed from his own character. The brash over-confidence of his acting and the prizefighter's way of emerging with poise from ridiculous situations had their counterpart in Flynn's life. In seven years with Warner Brothers, this was the closest he had come to doing what many falsely swore he did in every picture – play himself.

Seventeen years later, when he wrote *My Wicked, Wicked Ways,* the relief was to make an agreeable memory.

Errol's last three pictures, starting with *They Died With Their Boots On,* had been directed by Raoul Walsh, who, though he was nearly twenty years Flynn's senior and was called 'Uncle' by the younger man, became a close friend. A distinguished film-maker whose output was to include the classic gangster-movie *White Heat,* Walsh had, as well as his professional gifts, exactly the sort of multi-faceted personality and colourful early life to appeal to Errol. Besides having been a movie-pioneer who became assistant to D. W. Griffith in 1912, 'Uncle' Walsh was a former stunt-rider and an ex-athlete, and he had done some acting, too. He worked with Griffith on *The Birth of a Nation* and afterwards went to Mexico to make a picture about Pancho Villa – the start of a career that was to result in two hundred films. Surviving Errol, he would make his last movie in 1964, but at the age of eighty-five, this remarkable man became a novelist with *Days of Wrath,* a Western so far available only in a French translation. Like the great Michael Curtiz, whom he had replaced as Errol Flynn's Number One Director, Raoul Walsh was to be first passed over by film historians and critics and then to attain the dubious distinction of becoming a cult-figure in the 'seventies. To Errol, though only one of them was his friend, both directors were supreme professionals who, though he might occasionally jib at their discipline, would unfailingly present him at his best on the screen.

During these years in the early 'forties, Errol had built himself Mulholland House, overlooking the San Fernando Valley. Hugely expensive and hugging the side of a hill, this bachelor-pad that he extended and improved became virtually open-house for his friends and hangers-on. In its original conception, Mulholland House might have been comparatively cheap, but as Errol altered and enlarged it, his new home came to cost $125,000. Of course, many of the guests were female, and it is worth remarking that, women like Lupe Velez aside, his conquests were not so much with his peers, the glamorous Hollywood sex-symbols, as with girls who were essentially working-class – car-hops, waitresses and stenographers.

The distinction is a facile one and yet real. It was to cost Errol dearly.

He never denied that he used his status as a star to get women. But it would have taken an expert to decide, in any given liaison, who was using whom. He turned his attentions, the available evidence indicates, much less to female stars than to starlets who were eager to get ahead by any route, including – and often especially – the bed. Errol could and occasionally did help them, but he repudiated the notion that this was a vicious commercial traffic: the relationships frequently ended in friendship, seldom with rancour.

There were many techniques for getting girls. One of them, with variation of their roles, was practised by Errol together with Raoul Walsh. Seeing an attractive woman, the star would appear stunned, with a gesture hastily summon the nearby-lurking Walsh and seek his reaction, whereupon the director, playing along, would say, "Of course, you're dead right. You mean for the part of the sister?" Thus the girl would believe that interest in her was *bona fide* and professional, and it was a fast method – if unethical – of establishing rapport. Usually, the device worked well, but occasionally results were "disastrous".

Among those whose careers Errol helped was Linda Christian, whom he claimed to have "discovered" in a Mexico City bar where he was drinking with Freddie McEvoy. She was Blanca Rosa Welter then – Mexican born, but possibly of Dutch and German extraction. She was a beautiful girl with reddish-brown hair, and she spoke good English. Thinking she might well make the grade as a Hollywood actress, Errol had her under a six-month contract at a salary of one hundred dollars per week plus expenses. As she needed some trifling cosmetic-dental work, he sent her for the improvement to his own dentist – only to be faced with a staggering bill. When Errol asked for details, he was told that she had had all her teeth capped at his expense.

He thought up the name Linda Fortune for her and was inordinately happy about it until John Barrymore guffawed at the humour of 'Miss Fortune'. Then Errol recalled his own loose associations with the *Bounty*. In the end, she was named after Fletcher Christian, leader of the famous mutiny.

Ironically, Linda Christian was to marry Tyrone Power – over at Fox Studios, the nearest thing Errol had to a swashbuckling rival.

At Mulholland House, Errol enjoyed, as always, the company of men like Bruce Cabot and Bud Ernst, though he admitted that more than a few questionable characters "wended their way up the hill to Mulholland". One of them, arguably, was the actor John Barrymore, who, already far gone with alcoholism, came to stay for three weeks before his death in 1942. Errol was to describe that period as "the most frightening three weeks I had since I was in the New Guinea jungle". David Niven never shared Flynn's liking for Barrymore, largely because "the great profile" smelled pungently, and even Errol found some of his habits hard to take, not least that of urinating out of the windows. When his host complained that he had taken the varnish off one of the picture-windows, Barrymore obligingly turned his attention to the fireplace. "The smell through the room," said Errol, "was atrocious."

There was a lesson here, though Errol seemed unwilling or unable to learn it.

In John Barrymore he might well have seen prefigured his own career, since he was probably already swilling vodka, difficult to detect on the breath or with tomato juice, in alarming quantities. That he perceived no awful warning might have had something to do with Errol's growing conviction that he would burn out fast. John Barrymore, living to be sixty, exceeded Flynn's life-span by a decade.

My Wicked, Wicked Ways contains an anecdote about the aftermath of Barrymore's death that is as hard to believe as it is grotesque. The wake at his passing being over, Errol returned to his home and let himself in, turning on the lights. They revealed Barrymore's corpse propped up in Flynn's favourite chair – at which sight Errol turned tail and ran, only to be stopped by his friends, Raoul Walsh among them, explaining that he had been the victim of a gag.

Some gag.

It was well within the brutal spirit of the practical jokes perpetrated by the Flynn set, but the difficulties, if it was really carried out, must have been enormous, and it was unlikely that the body, as Errol asserted, could have been smuggled out of the Pierce Brothers Mortuary on Sunset Boulevard.

His feelings about Barrymore might have been more than tinged with ambivalence, but Errol had the greatest personal as well as professional regard for Alan Hale, whom he feared as the biggest scene-stealer in the business. In films or theatre, the practice is really a form of bad manners, but Hale and Flynn were kindred spirits, so that scene-stealing was a kind of game to them, even if they never practised it on each other. Errol, however, learned many of the tricks from his friend.

My Wicked, Wicked Ways contains an excellent story about Hale and S. Z. 'Cuddles' Sakall, each of whom hated the other. Sakall, the heavy-jowled, bespectacled Hungarian comic-support of so many films of those years, was notorious for his distortions of the English language – which were naturally used for comedy in his pictures. Errol brought the two together one night at Mulholland – "a meeting of two prima donnas at a tea-party".

Hale yelled at Sakall, "For Chrissakes, Sakall, ain't it time you learned to speak English? You been here long enough!"

Sakall replied, "And for vy I should spik English better, ven mitt dis Englich I em making more vot is you!"

Another frequent visitor to Errol's luxury-house was Freddie McEvoy, whom he had known in Australia and England. Physically well endowed for the part, McEvoy was a self-professed sportsman and international adventurer, out to make a rich marriage, and it was he who introduced to Errol, Alexandre, who became the star's valet and ran Mulholland. (The information supplied by Errol that Alexandre was an ex-Russian royalist man-servant should be received with scepticism.) People called Freddie McEvoy 'Tiger', perhaps because of the effect created by piercing blue eyes but equally probably because of his strength.

When he and Errol fought once, the cause of the quarrel McEvoy's attempt to keep his friend off opium, Flynn stayed out of trouble only through speed and dancing feet, though both he and his opponent ended up on the ground in a state of collapse.

The two friends, Alan Hale and Freddie McEvoy were to pre-decease Errol – Hale somewhat prematurely at fifty-eight and McEvoy, after twenty years of comradeship with the star, trying to save his wife after their yacht had broken up in a storm off the coast of Western Africa. In a dubious epitaph, Errol said that this gesture was essentially out of character for the selfish Freddie he had known. When the drowned body was eventually found, it was unrecognizable except by the gold buckle on a belt. He had swiped that buckle from Errol.

The bachelor-husband believed that he had worked out a reasonable arrangement with Lili Damita, but she was yet to surprise him – and not by hurling something at him, a practice to which Errol had become accustomed. On one of his visits to her apartment, she announced that she was pregnant. As reported, the actual words were: "Fleen, you think you've screwed every dame in Hollywood, but now I've screwed you, my friend. You will have a child!"

No wonder he called her Tiger Lil.

Sean Flynn was born on 10th May 1941, and his father loved the idea of having a son.

Lili, too, had got what she wanted, and she and Errol were divorced in 1942 with what he categorized as "the most brutal property settlement ever made". (She received $1,500 a month and a half-interest in all he owned.) He might have been happy enough about the terms at the time, but Lili never remarried during Flynn's lifetime, and the constant drain of her alimony on his finances was no doubt crippling in the long run, if not immediately. As Errol wrote bitterly, "Even if I worked all my life exclusively for her, I could never meet the tax on the tax on the tax."

However, in the short term, he had much greater worries.

In 1942 he was working on *Edge of Darkness* when one night his valet Alexandre came into his study at Mulholland House to say that two plain-clothes policemen were at the door. Alexandre was shaking, and Errol, amused, told him to show the men in, not thinking at the time that *two* policemen were usually a bad sign.

They had come, they said, to take a statement from Errol, and when he asked what it was all about, they summed up the matter in two words: "Statutory rape".

7

Edge of Darkness

It could have been another of those crude practical jokes his friends were so fond of, but Errol knew it was not.

He was not even sure of the difference between rape and statutory rape, but he had the sense to call his lawyer, Robert Ford, before he accompanied the officers to Juvenile Hall, where Ford met him. When the lawyer asked what the idea was of bringing his client down there, the policeman explained that the accuser and the accused must confront each other.

The 'accuser' turned out to be seventeen-year-old Betty Hansen – "that frowsy little blonde", as Errol called her. He knew her, and he was in big trouble, all right.

Bit by bit, a case against him was assembled, and in purely technical terms it looked bad – bad enough for Errol to retain Jerry Giesler, the crack trial-lawyer whose career was to include the defence of Robert Mitchum on drugs-charges, Charles Chaplin on charges of violation of the Mann Act, and Cheryl Crane, Lana Turner's daughter, in a hearing that resulted in a verdict of justifiable homicide. (In *My Wicked, Wicked Ways,* Errol and his collaborator did the late Giesler the honour of misspelling his name no fewer than twenty times.)

Giesler was a brilliant defence-attorney – the sort of label he much preferred to the term 'criminal lawyer'. Though he was capable of histrionics and emotional appeals to juries, he defeated his opponents in court as much through careful preparation before the trial as by any other more spectacular tactic. He excelled in representing Hollywood celebrities such as Robert Mitchum, whom he advised to plead guilty to narcotics offences – a deft public-relations manoeuvre that reduced publicity to a minimum by sidestepping a lengthy public trial. However, Giesler repudiated the notion that he was celebrity-orientated, arguing that his skill lay in persuading juries that his famous clients, once they were in the harsh exposure of a court of law, were ordinary human beings with recognizable problems. A proper man, a professed conservative, Giesler nevertheless harboured a sneaking affection for Errol Flynn. Giesler, who was born in Iowa in 1886, as a young man hero-worshipped the famous Clarence Darrow, and after graduation, he was associated with Earl Rogers, the renowned criminal lawyer. Deceptively quiet in the courtroom, Giesler grew quieter with age. Though he was vastly different from Flynn, he was to say of him: "Errol was a lovable character, but his own worst enemy. He was made up of many fine parts you don't find in the ordinary person. Although he often gave the appearance of being a cynic, there was sentimental side to him. He was a very sweet character."

When the case blew up, Errol's memories of Betty Hansen were probably vague at best. What had happened to result in the visit from the two policemen seemed relatively simple. After her sister had reported her as a missing person, Betty was taken into police-custody. Routine interrogation produced the names of several men with whom she had had sexual relationships, Flynn among them. To lend credibility to her story, Errol's unlisted telephone-number was in her possession.

From these beginnings emerged the charge of statutory rape, but in October the Grand Jury of Los Angeles County, given the facts, returned with a 'No True Bill': there would be no indictment of Errol Flynn.

Not yet.

Errol came to believe that the LA District Attorney, morally vengeful towards Hollywood, had decided to make an example of him, Flynn. Detectives working out of the DA's office were looking for evidence against the star, and in the hope of overriding the Grand Jury decision, they dug up from files in a sheriff's office a complaint that Errol had raped a legal minor on the *Sirocco.*

The girl's name was Peggy La Rue Satterlee, and a medical examination at the time her mother made the complaint revealed that Peggy had indeed been brutally violated.

Why, then, had the sheriff's office allowed months to elapse and done nothing?

Whatever the explanation (and a satisfactory one was not found), the District Attorney decided to move against Flynn – this time, levelling both barrels at him: the Hansen charge backed up by the Satterlee charge. In Errol's own words: "Somebody was out to put the screws on me."

Jerry Giesler agreed, smelling dirty politics. He was also to observe that the complainants were "quite the sophisticates, wise in the ways of the world". There appeared to be at least one other strange angle to the case, summed up by Errol's statement: "To this day nobody knows for certain how old Peggy Satterlee was; although it appeared later, from a driver's licence she owned, that she was twenty-one." If so, it was not the sort of point Giesler would overlook. Nor did he. Peggy often exaggerated her age to get work, and she did so to obtain the licence, too – a fact of which Giesler made devastating use, especially exploiting its implication of habitual falsehood. (As so often, Errol, when he came to write his biography, dragged up a confused, blurred and even illogical memory.)

For Errol, much was at stake – not to put it too strongly, his whole life and career. If he was indicted and convicted, the second would virtually be over, the moralists dancing on its grave. As for his life, a 'guilty'-verdict would carry a prison-term, and in the event of non-acquittal, Errol had arranged for a private 'plane to fly him out of the country.

At the preliminary hearing on 2nd November 1942, Assistant District Attorney Thomas W. Cochran put Betty Hansen on the stand to testify to an encounter with Errol at a Bel Air party, during which, after they had come to know each other, they had retired to an upstairs bedroom.

Errol could not have denied that he knew well the scene of the alleged crime. It was a Mediterranean-style mansion on St Pierre Road, Bel Air, and the two-storey structure with red-tiled roof had rambling grounds in which were to be found a tennis-court and swimming-pool. Other sports were catered for indoors – and not only the one in which Errol was supposed to have committed a foul. There was a great deal of betting and card-playing, so that Errol, with friends who always seemed to win, claimed that his own visits were expensive. (One of them was certainly to prove so.) In later decades, such a place would automatically have been referred to as a bachelor-pad, and this one, having formerly belonged to the silent star Colleen Moore, was at that time rented by Bruce Cabot, Stephen Raphael and Freddie McEvoy – three of the colony's most swinging bachelors.

"There were always lovely girls around," Errol admitted.

He could not deny, either, that he had met Betty Hansen there, though she scarcely qualified as one of the lovely girls. On the contrary, she was a shy, unmemorable person who, as the trial was to reveal, spoke poor, ungrammatical English. ("I didn't have no objections" was her most quoted solecism. If we were to assume that Errol did indeed make love to her, she was certainly not outside his range of preference, strange though that fact might seem. The man who could presumably have had the pick of the available women – some of the most beautiful in the world – all too often sought merely youth and acquiescence.)

This mousy character was now to be instrumental in putting Errol through the greatest ordeal of his life.

The court-transcript of the preliminary hearing shows the following exchange between the Assistant DA and his star-witness:

COCHRAN: Then what did Mr. Flynn do?
HANSEN: He undressed me.
C.: Forcibly?
H.: Forcibly.
C.: Using his superior strength?
H.: He was quite determined.
C.: Did you help undress yourself?
H.: No.
C.: Did he remove all your clothing?
H.: All, except my shoes and stockings.
C.: And then what happened?
H.: He undressed himself.
C.: Did he remove all his clothing?
H.: Everything except his shoes.
C.: What happened next?

H.: We, well –
C.: What happened next, Miss Hansen?
H.: We had an act of intercourse.
C.: You state that you had an act of sexual intercourse with Mr Flynn right there in that upstairs bedroom?
H.: Yes.
C.: And this act was forced on you. I mean to say, it was against your will?
H.: It was against my will.
C.: When you said before that you had an act of sexual intercourse with Mr Flynn – you meant, didn't you, that Mr Flynn inserted his private parts into your private parts?
H.: Yes.
C.: Please speak up so everybody can hear you, Miss Hansen.
H.: Yes, it was like that.
C.: How long would you say the act of sexual intercourse took?
H.: A half hour. Maybe fifty minutes.

If the utterance of this testimony was distressing for Betty Hansen, it can be imagined that Errol, with his strong feelings about privacy, loathed it.

To prevent an indictment, Jerry Giesler, predictably, sought to destroy Betty Hansen's credibility. If this was a familiar tactic, it also had an ethical impulse: the lawyer thought that the girl was a hustler – out to make what capital she could from the case against his client and never innocent or naïve in the first place.

Her innocence or the lack of it, though, were essentially irrelevant to the legal issue – immaterial to the charge against Errol, who had allegedly made love with a *minor.* Nor had the prosecution actually charged that Errol employed violence during the episode. For the same reason, there was no need: consent or the lack of it did not affect the case.

Even so, Giesler did a good job of showing up the girl as somewhat less than pure. He first established – damagingly – that someone had advised Betty to begin a deliberate campaign to involve herself with Errol and that she had done so eagerly enough.

GIESLER: I asked, did you think that if you acted friendly to

Mr Flynn and he liked you, he then might be helpful to you?

HANSEN: Yes, in a way I thought that.

G.: Did you think that?

H.: Yes, I thought that.

G.: That Mr Flynn would do what he could to get you a job?

H.: I might have thought like that.

G.: I'd like a more specific answer, Miss Hansen.

H.: I thought Mr Flynn might help me.

G.: Get a job?

H.: Get a job.

G.: You were of course aware that he was a motion picture actor, and had some influence?

H.: Yes, I was.

G.: Speak up, Miss Hansen, so we all can hear.

H.: Yes, I was.

G.: Aware of Mr Flynn's status and influence as a motion picture star?

H.: I was aware of that, yes.

G.: You, in fact, liked him. I mean, prior to actually meeting him in person. You'd seen him in pictures in your home town, and you liked him.

H.: No, I didn't like him.

G.: You didn't.

H.: No, I didn't. I didn't think much of his acting.

G.: Is this in his pictures? Are you referring to his acting in pictures?

H.: Yes, in pictures. I seen some of his pictures, and I didn't like his acting.

Giesler's reiterative, wearing, jabbing technique secured other damaging admissions: she had made no protest when Errol locked the door of the bedroom; she had made no attempt to open it and escape; she was confused about whether the star had undressed her or whether she had undressed herself; she had resisted Errol only by telling him to stop.

Thus Betty Hansen's performance as star-witness was in effect ridiculed by Errol's lawyer, but Jerry Giesler knew that his cross-examination had won a battle, at best – not the war. There was still the incontrovertible fact that the girl was a minor. He could hope only that her story would be totally disbelieved.

The hearing then turned its attention to the testimony of Peggy La Rue Satterlee, who alleged that Errol had twice forced himself upon her as her host on the *Sirocco.*

Unlike Betty Hansen, Peggy Satterlee *was* beautiful, and Errol Flynn *might* therefore have made love to her. Although she was only sixteen at the time of the trial, she looked, despite attempts to disguise her mature aura, at least five years older – an appearance she exploited in getting jobs. She frequently posed as twenty-one, and she had had work in nightclubs as a showgirl. With a good figure, lustrous dark hair and green eyes, she could not have escaped Errol's notice if he had ever met her.

And he had.

There was more juicy evidence, little of it too convincing, especially since after the alleged violation on the *Sirocco,* during which she had neither struggled nor cried out, she stayed on board enjoying herself – not to say making herself available for the next seduction.

This took place in a cabin, where she looked at the moon through a porthole – an unfortunate gratuitous detail provided by Miss Satterlee, because the moon that night was on the *other* side of the *Sirocco.* Giesler was to make much of this invention in the trial at the Los Angeles County Superior Court.

Her allegations, though improbable, were serious, and she proved less easy to manipulate than Betty Hansen.

GIESLER: Did Mr Flynn insert his privates into you?
SATTERLEE: Yes.
G.: While he did that, were you fighting him or in any way resisting?
S.: Yes, I was.
G.: He was able to complete the act even though you were resisting?
S.: Yes.

Having submitted meekly to Errol on the first occasion, she testified, Peggy Satterlee was hardly one for consistent behaviour, it seemed. But Giesler, though his work had been more brilliant than most realized, was not successful in stopping the proceedings at this point, and Errol was indicted.

However, the trial on three counts of statutory rape soon showed who knew about trials and juries and who did not.

The case was heard in January 1943 in the Los Angeles County Superior Court, where Giesler got off to a fine start by making sure that no fewer than nine women were on the jury. Then, with Betty Hansen and Peggy Satterlee more or less repeating their earlier testimony, Giesler went into action with *argumentum ad hominem*: he not so much countered the charges as demolished all those associated with them and their motives for bringing or being involved in the case. For example, he at last succeeded in introducing evidence of Betty Hansen's earlier sex-life and, by innuendo, attacked Peggy Satterlee.

Having laid the groundwork at the earlier hearing, he battered the prosecution's case by deriding the palpably untrue embellishment of the moon peering in at the porthole as Errol did his dastardly deed. Summing up to the jury, Giesler impugned the *motives* of both girls: to avoid prosecution themselves on other matters, they were allowing themselves to be used as cat's-paws in a conspiracy against Flynn.

Errol had to take the stand. (Not by legal requirement, but Giesler must have decided there was little choice in a pragmatic sense. In any event, he probably knew his jury by then.) Errol swore that he had been gallant, but no more than that – on his own yacht, merely a chivalrous host; and his appearance in the witness-box no doubt went straight to the hearts – not the minds – of those women-jurors. Peggy La Rue Satterlee commented: "I knew those women on the jury would acquit him. They just sat there and looked at him adoringly just like he was their son or something."

In short, Giesler won the case.

If not a victory for truth, the verdict was at least a victory for commonsense and a morality higher than legal technicalities and the savage demands of conventional rectitude. That Errol should have been prosecuted at all was viciously unfair; that the proceedings should have been bulldozed to this point revealed enormous malice in whoever plotted against him.

For once, justice rather than law had prevailed.

But what of Errol during all this legal manoeuvring?

One courtroom reporter wrote, "Flynn's eyes were red-speckled, unslept, and his cheeks were chalk. His smile was patent, false. There were strings in his face, taut and extruded. More than anyone else in the courtroom, Flynn knew exactly what was at stake. His future. Even perhaps his life." The physical description might have been slightly exaggerated, since contemporary photographs, if they do not reveal the customary dapper Errol Flynn, at least show him grave but controlled.

With the rest, one can only agree.

Of course the trial had its comic aspects, such as the sight of the innocent Peggy Satterlee in bobbysocks and pigtails. But the defendant was in no mood to savour them fully. He had been pinning all on Jerry Giesler, whom he described as "a man with force, but with no overbearing personality. His power lay in his latent strength".

One omission by his attorney had mildly perturbed Errol.

"Jerry Giesler never asked me whether I was guilty or innocent. Not once in . . . the five months of trial operations. Maybe he was afraid I was guilty, and didn't want to know it." The matter was not clarified when Giesler told him that Flynn was the best witness he had ever had. In such a context, with Errol a professional actor, "best" was an ambiguous term.

When the verdict was announced, there was applause in court, and Errol's embrace made Giesler turn red with embarrassment. Judge Leslie E. Stills said to the jury: "I think you have arrived at a proper verdict." Perhaps unmindful – if only temporarily – of what the trial had done to the defendant, he added, "I have enjoyed the case, and I think you have." Naturally, the star was not wearing a hat, but – ever gallant – Errol Flynn touched his hair to the ladies.

When it was all over, in a superb moment of unconscious irony, Betty Hansen's mother remarked, "Oh, well, nobody got hurt."

To understand what the ordeal had meant and done to

Errol, it is necessary to know something of the effect of major trials upon defendants. No less an authority than Judge Learned Hand has said, "I must say that, as a litigant, I should dread a lawsuit beyond almost anything short of sickness and death." To which it might be added that lengthy and important trials not infrequently *lead* to sickness and premature death. If there is anything considerable at stake, the strain is enormous. Anyone who has studied the histories of such proceedings and their aftermaths must have been struck by how often the defendant, following an acquittal, fails to recover physically or psychologically, occasionally even dying soon afterwards, so that the trial and its stresses might be construed as having shortened his life. In his book *The Defence Never Rests,* the renowned lawyer F. Lee Bailey writes of one of his most famous clients, "It had taken me a long time to realize it, but when Sam Sheppard got out of jail, he was a condemned man. Nothing could put him back into a personality that would last. He won his freedom, and he won exoneration. But he couldn't win back his life."

Of course, Errol Flynn had not been to jail, and his testing had been slight compared with that of Sheppard, who had been tried for murder. Errol had not actually been on trial for his life – not literally. But he had been taken to a police-station and fingerprinted. He had suffered the agonies of protracted legal proceedings and doubt about their outcome. This had been among the most stringent of ordeals, and though he was thirty-four and was to live for another sixteen years, there can be no doubt that he never recovered from the stress.

The courtroom experience was bad enough. Errol's cross-examination had gone on for hour after hour, session after session, though the accused had actually been seen to grow stronger and more confident under this barrage of questioning. He had heard his own counsel ask him, "Did you make this statement to (Peggy Satterlee)? Did you say, 'Since I had possession of you once, you might as well let me again.'?" He had listened to prosecution-speeches describing him as a "sex criminal" and "ravisher of little girls". Even the verdict had not been swift and automatic: the jury, having been locked up overnight, had technically been out for over twenty-four hours. By the time they returned, Errol's complexion had a yellow tinge, and his eyes were bloodshot.

But the courtroom was only part of his ordeal. The newspapers had been full of the proceedings, and Errol had had to contend not only with his feelings of humiliation but also his dread of what his parents would think. For his mother's reaction, he might have cared comparatively little; but he had always valued Professor Flynn's approval.

Furthermore, he was soon to have proof of his social standing within the Hollywood colony. Soon – too soon – after he was acquitted, he invited lots of people to a party, but he reported that hardly anyone came.

Even deprived of the verdict they craved, the moralists had had a field-day, and the law had examined matters that Errol deemed entirely private. He realized that, for all his apparent victory, he had lost: "I knew that I could never escape this brand that was now upon me: that I would always be associated in the public mind with an internationally followed rape case." Although his box-office appeal observably increased after the trial, Errol dated his decline from that time. Women, he asserted, preyed on him, though "I yielded with a smile to the now complete legend of myself as a modern Don Juan."

He did more than that. He actually worked at it. Towards the end of his life, he wrote, "I hate the legend of myself as a phallic representation, yet I work at it to keep it alive."

He was aware that if he had not been one before, he had now become a joke. His publicity, always fierce, now became a blinding glare in which simple living was almost impossible. Entirely sympathetic to the star, yet helping to make him a caricature, US servicemen coined the jocular phrase to describe an easy amorous conquest: "In like Flynn". The saying was to persist for many years. (If it ever fell into disuse, it was revived in the late 'sixties by the punning title of a James Coburn movie, *In Like Flint.*) There were many other jokes. Milton Berle was to quip subtly, "Youth must have its Flynn." Another saying that did the rounds was: "My name's Flynn. What's *your* hobby?" Testimony had revealed that on one occasion Errol had kept his socks on to make love, and so some wag suggested that the roughly contemporary *Gentleman Jim* should be retitled plain *Jim.* When *They Died With Their Boots On* was released, the film's title seemed to be a joke in itself.

Errol suffered the joke, made the best of it. In urbane mood, he once said, "The public has always expected me to be a playboy, and a decent chap never lets his public down. I'll live this half of my life. I don't care about the other half."

He had lost, too, in a more mundane way. To Errol, the cost of the trial was $50,000, of which $30,000 went directly to Giesler, the rest being for his expenses. (These are Errol's own figures; another source states that he paid $75,000.) By the standards of Giesler, who reportedly charged Charles Chaplin $100,000, the fee was not particularly high.

But money, important though it was, represented only part of the bill, the balance being exacted less tangibly but more seriously through spiritual and psychological depletion.

Errol was deeply scarred.

The best was over.

8

Footsteps in the Dark

Somehow, life goes on, even in the middle of a rape-trial.

Errol completed *Edge of Darkness* (1943), finely directed by Lewis Milestone. The actor gave a restrained performance that, in its under-stated way, was among his best, and then did a song-and-dance number in David Butler's all-star musical *Thank Your Lucky Stars.* It was almost as though he was cocking a snook at fate. As a cockney sailor with walrus moustache, he sang and hoofed his way through "That's What You Jolly Well Get" in a London pub in which he was obviously known as a rogue. This brief appearance might have been uncharacteristic but it revealed once more the deft comedy talents of Flynn that were never to be fully explored. Furthermore, since the cockney sailor was full of tales of phoney heroics, Errol might well have experienced some sort of therapy in satirizing his more usual screen-personality, especially as he was by that time deeply into the celluloid cycle of World War II bravery.

However, Errol not only continued working during the rape-trial but also embarked upon what was to be – though he did not realize it then – the prelude to his second marriage.

During his constant visits to the Hall of Justice, he had noticed an attractive redhead who served behind the cigar-stand. Her name was Nora Eddington, and her job was only temporary, as relief-worker for a six-week period. The case on his mind, Errol made a cautious check and discovered that Nora was eighteen and therefore not jailbait. What he did not at first know was that she was the daughter of Captain Jack Eddington of the Los Angeles County Sheriff's Office.

Nora's mother had been Mexican. She had married while very young, and her husband's family did not approve of the union, which broke up almost immediately, but not before

Nora had been conceived. As a result, she was brought up by her Mexican grandmother until she was nine, speaking only Spanish for the first seven years. Because of this early history, Errol's pet-names for her included "peon" and "wetback".

For her part, the grown-up Nora could hardly have failed to be aware of the presence of Errol Flynn in the Hall of Justice, but having seen him, she did not at first consider him so special.

Errol moved cautiously. Instead of making a direct approach, he had a stuntman-friend of his, Buster Wiles, arrange for her to visit Mulholland House. (This device – using what is sometimes called a 'beard' – was a favourite with Errol, who was later to employ the same tactic with Beverly Aadland.) Wiles was a charmer, but Nora was uncertain about the arrangement, and so it was agreed that she should be accompanied by a girlfriend, who, even if she could not neutralize the Flynn chemistry, would at least satisfy the demands of propriety. In his own expensive setting, Errol made a much stronger impression than he had made at the Hall of Justice. Nora found him by the pool, dressed in white gabardine slacks and little else, and she has recorded that "his head seemed sculptured, the profile flawless" and that the star was "graceful in movement and lithe and sleek as a well-cared-for-animal". The description might well be contrasted with that of the courtroom-reporter recorded at approximately the same time. (The apparent contradiction is easy to explain. Before approaching Nora, Errol had waited until *after* his trial, and though the intervening period might have been comparatively short, his acquittal had helped him shed or begin to shed whatever signs of strain the reporter had observed.)

Next day, Nora was invited to dinner. Raoul Walsh was there with his wife and daughter, Errol obviously taking pains to reassure a young and undoubtedly nervous girl, and afterwards they went to the preview of *Edge of Darkness.* Later, Nora and Errol went on alone to the Mocambo, where Nora, troubled by the drift of events, at last blurted out that she was a virgin and had no intention of sleeping with him.

If the news alarmed Errol, he gave no sign and was certainly not deterred. His most obvious response seems to have been to employ her as his secretary - a step that solved the problem of their dates together cutting into her working-hours at Lockheed, for she had by then finished the cigar-stand job. What she was actually doing was helping Errol with work on his novel *Showdown,* which was to be published a couple of years later.

At this time, he was still dating other girls, and flocks of people visited the house at weekends, for which Nora and he sometimes went away. When they did, they had separate rooms.

They were getting to know each other well, even if the ultimate sexual intimacy had yet to take place, and there were two traits Nora disliked about Errol. One was his drinking, though if her report is reliable, the daily intake did not then begin until late afternoon. The other was his penchant for practical jokes, about which Errol, by his own admission, had a curious philosophy. He reserved these pranks for his friends, not his enemies, and such cruelty as he had was channelled into the type of hoax that always, analysis would reveal, had a substratum of malice. He seemed unaware of that cruel streak, perhaps always having taken the merry japes for granted since his early years, when, as a man among men, he had formed so many attitudes that ill fitted him for sharing his life with women.

In her book *Errol and Me,* Nora Eddington has given us a vivid picture of the star's life-style both before and after their marriage, and it is on that source that much of the material that follows is based. Errol himself was strangely reticent about the marriage, both at first, when he was reluctant to admit to it, and years later when he came to write *My Wicked, Wicked Ways,* in whose pages there are only a few short paragraphs on the subject.

When Nora first knew him, Errol's group of real friends was kept separate from his casual girlfriends. Nora realized that after she left the house in the evening, Errol often had girls and men there, and she did not question what went on. Though he did not pay for sex for himself, he would supply 'professionals' for his guests.

Their relationship was resolved somewhat abruptly after a party at which Errol had pressed a great deal of wine on her. Whether he had planned to or not (and it might be presumed that his impatience had at least kept pace with his interest in Nora), he made love to her that night. With some reluctance and the knowledge that he was still seeing other women, she afterwards agreed to become his mistress – though Errol had two others whom he saw as often as he saw her. "He was changing women," Nora wrote, "as fast as Alex [his valet] could change the sheets."

Alexandre was in what some might have considered a privileged situation, since he got the leavings from the table and the bed. One of Errol's girls was a New York model who tried to commit suicide at Mulholland – at which point Errol told her flatly that he had had enough. In order to be near him, she began sleeping with Alex.

Nora had that sort of thing to endure and more besides. One day, she saw Errol in the bathroom with a hypodermic. What he was doing was obvious enough, but when she mentioned addiction, he laughed at the idea, defending his right to try everything once.

He might have added, "And again and again and again..."

When Nora discovered she was pregnant, Errol's response was to talk about abortion, but at length he agreed to marry her – since she was determined to have the child – so that the infant would be legitimate. It was agreed that they would divorce afterwards and that Nora would claim nothing except seventy-five dollars a week child-support. The marriage was to be kept secret.

With a girlfriend, Nora went off to Mexico City, where she was to have the baby. While she was there, Errol's friends Freddie and Puppy McEvoy, in on the secret, visited her frequently. She needed people to keep her spirits up, because she read in the newspapers that Errol was dating her cousin. When he finally turned up, it was without warning and the pregnancy was well advanced. Lines of dissipation showed in his face, and Nora became suspicious about visits to the bathroom after which Errol re-emerged rolling down one sleeve. While he was out for a drink, she searched his suitcase until she found a hypodermic, a bent spoon and drugs.

The facts spoke for themselves.

The meaning Nora gave to them was probably close to what anyone might presume long after the events: Errol's growing dependence on drugs and alcohol was at least partly a symptom of the aftermath of his trial for rape. She said that he took drugs because he needed 'a lift' – in his case, from the depths of depression.

He and Nora were married by proxy in Cuernavaca. The next day, Errol left, promising to return for the birth of the child.

In *My Wicked, Wicked Ways,* he stated that they were married "a few months after the trial", but since their daughter, Deirdre, was born on 10th January 1945, not long after the marriage by Nora's account, Errol's chronology is as usual suspect. The marriage date was probably late autumn or early winter, 1944.

Whether to marry Nora, however, had been only one of his big problems that year. Another complication, particularly as it came so soon after his trial, was a threatened paternity-suit. The twenty-three-year-old wife of a sailor, Shirley Elaine Evans Hassau, alleged that Errol was the father of her three-year-old child. What she had in mind was explicit enough: a settlement of $1,750 a week.

Shirley Hassau was blonde and pretty, but when she claimed that Errol had made love to her in the front seat of a convertible coupé, he ridiculed the idea on the grounds that a man of his build, six foot two, would never have made love anywhere but in the back seat – and then only with the greatest discomfort in a coupé.

Despite the comedy, the allegation presented a threat, and he agreed to talk matters over with Mrs Hassau's parents in the office of his business-manager. They turned up with a three-year-old child with yellow curls and blue eyes. Errol denied that she could be his daughter. Possibly he wanted to fight the contention, but his manager proved persuasive, and he settled the case out of court for a mere $3,000 – cheap at the price.

His manager had been right. The potential nuisance-value

was enormous, and Jack Warner would have been in no mood to tolerate yet another Flynn scandal. Years later, when Tallulah Bankhead was being considered for a part in a film, someone broke the news to Warner that Miss Bankhead drank. Immediately, he killed the idea of putting her under contract, saying that he had had enough of that sort of thing with Flynn.

Errol's troubles might have damaged himself, but the various scandals and headaches did not do Jack Warner any good, either.

The rape case had crowded war news off the front pages, and with audiences more enthusiastic than ever, Warner Brothers and Errol were pushing ahead with his career. In 1943 and 1944, he made *Northern Pursuit* and *Uncertain Glory*, two indifferent war-movies. Then, in 1945, he made a picture he was to remember for the rest of his days.

Ironically, Errol described *Objective, Burma!* as "one of the few pictures of which I am proud", and it is not difficult to see what he had in mind. The film, strikingly directed by his close friend Raoul Walsh, has a documentary aura to it, and Errol was perhaps justifiably enthusiastic about the picture's authenticity and its assiduously simulated conditions of the Burma campaign. His own performance was straightforward and effective, its dimensions recognizably human. The truth is, though, that no matter how well crafted, the film was little more than light entertainment, the screenplay (by Ranald MacDougall and Lester Cole, after an Alvah Bessie original) being predictable and stereotyped.

It ran into trouble, however, on grounds that were not aesthetic, at least in England. Even today, hackles still rise at the mere mention of the picture. The furore at its original showing caused it to be withdrawn after playing only a week in a London cinema. It was alleged that *Objective, Burma!* inaccurately depicted the Americans alone invading Burma, the British being omitted by an unfortunate oversight.

"In [England]," Errol wrote, "which gave me my accent and my histrionic training and was my motherland until the time I took out American citizenship, you would have thought that I was the representative of the State Department in Washington, telling the British that not only were Americans winning World War II, but that I, Flynn, was doing it single-handed." The tone might have been flippant, but Errol was deeply upset that most of the blame seemed to be levelled at him personally, and the hurt was an enduring one.

Fortunately, *San Antonio* (1945), a handsomely mounted Western, produced no such problems. It was as enjoyable as it was unremarkable.

The news of Deirdre Flynn's birth did not remain a secret and soon hit the headlines. The press suspected a marriage, but Errol refused to confirm the hunch and left Nora in Mexico, until, after three months, she returned to her father's home and the marriage was admitted.

Errol appeared to be in no hurry to go through with a divorce as planned. There could, however, have been several reasons for his letting matters ride. He was already wary of divorce and its financial consequences in Southern California. His expenses were huge, and he had a career on which to concentrate. For all its dissatisfactions, real or imagined, that career gave his life some meaning and a focal point.

Furthermore, his marriage was not seriously interfering with his freedom. He bought Nora a house in Hollywood, where she lived while he carried on with his bachelor-existence at Mulholland. "This," he stated, "was the only way I would be married to anybody: separate house[s], separate lives, separate people." Even more astonishing – to an outsider, at any rate – was his installation of Marge Eddington, Nora's stepmother, as housekeeper at Mulholland.

Errol's life, though few folks seemed particularly interested in the facts, was not all women and good times, but as he confessed, "I gave a good performance as the guy who just doesn't give a damn." Always ambivalent in his attitude towards women, he became even more disillusioned about them during this period, and he was later, in his autobiography, to coin the *bon mot*: "The man who for a woman fits the bill is the one who pays the bill."

By his own account, he was "walking through" the films he made at this time, but since one of them was *Objective, Burma!*, his own pet project, the assertion must be regarded with some scepticism. His apathy, he said, was so infectious that David Butler, who directed *San Antonio,* took little care in the task. The finished picture – not one of the greatest ever to come out of Hollywood, but not one of the worst, either – offers no hard evidence to support Errol's statement.

"I wasn't much of a parent," he said, and yet the world's worst husband clearly had a feeling for children that comes across attractively in such films as *Kim* and *The Prince and the Pauper.* In 1957, when he sued *Confidential* magazine for libel, the step seemed surprising from "the guy who just [didn't] give a damn". But Errol explained that he did it for his children ("these little ones"), who had been made to suffer unfairly.

So, by two marriages, he had his little ones, though it may be guessed that he did not spend too much time with them. He had the career that now appeared so stale to him – but lucrative. And he had the strange arrangement with Nora (and Marge Eddington) that he called marriage and of which he was to write: "Candidly, life with the Eddingtons, Nora and her stepmother, provided no pattern for the human race on which to model itself in any effort towards fashioning the perfect home."

Once more, Errol was about to be saved from his own lethargy and low spirits by his love of the sea. Throughout his life that love sustained him during the blackest periods. When he considered himself washed up in the 'fifties, it offered nourishment until his career picked up with *Istanbul.* His knowledge of ships might have been more limited than he cared to admit, but "the lure of the sea, in all its forms," he said, "is probably the strongest urge in me."

In the mid-'forties, he was at a low ebb, during which he sat on the bed for hours with a revolver, contemplating suicide. From this depression, he snapped out to some degree by buying a new boat. The *Sirocco* was a disturbing reminder of the rape-case, and in a new craft, the *Zaca,* Errol sought peace. (He must have found the name – a Samoan word meaning precisely that – especially attractive.) He spent $50,000 to have the *Zaca* refitted. She was a two-masted schooner that had been used by the navy in World War II, having originally belonged to a San Francisco banker, and Errol saw the possibility of converting her into his dream-boat.

By the time that dream had come true, his mother and father were in America on a visit. His mother had two grandchildren in Los Angeles to fuss over – the tiny Deirdre and the much older Sean. It was Errol's plan to leave her to it and take off with his father on the *Zaca* to the Galapagos Islands.

They set sail in August 1946.

Among those on board, there were another scientist, Professor Carl Hubbs, Errol's friend John Decker and Wallace Beery Jr. Nora went along, too, and she and Decker got along so badly that he left the ship at Acapulco. Nora also did, though not ostensibly because of social dislocation. She was pregnant again, and the risks of sailing were too great for her to continue.

The evidence, however, suggests that her departure was not entirely unconnected with the strained relationship between her and the artist John Decker, though it has to be admitted that only one of them needed to leave the *Zaca* to clear the air.

Trouble began when Errol gave Nora the unenviable task of being custodian of the icebox – a small affair that contained only three icetrays. Decker, who was fond of liberal quantities of ice in his drinks, did not respond well to the idea of asking his hostess to unlock the precious supplies, and he nicknamed her 'Captain Bligh'.

Matters grew worse as an indirect result of the scarcity of fresh water. The method was not very satisfactory, but crew and guests would take their baths over the side in a canvas swing – a procedure that Decker declined when his turn came. Jesting, Errol warned him that he, Flynn, was the captain, and the captain's word was law: even artists were not exempt from taking baths. In the end, the joke was carried to the point of tossing Decker, fully clothed, over the side. He did not take the episode in good spirit, and having seen Nora whispering to a half-drunk Errol just before the horseplay, he blamed her, though the idea had been Errol's.

Decker finally alienated Nora by proposing to paint her

family coat of arms – "crossed ice cubes with the refrigerator keys frozen inside". Later on, at Acapulco, he had a sort of revenge by giving the Los Angeles newspapers stories in which Nora figured unfavourably and was said to be known, according to Decker, all over Mexico as "*Capitán Sangre*" (the Spanish for "Captain Blood").

Besides internal strife among the guests, the trip was marred by other mishaps, such as Beery getting a harpoon in his left foot – an accident for which Errol offers no explanation in *My Wicked, Wicked Ways.* But Errol was back with his first love, "equal to Ulysses and brother to him", and the farther away from Hollywood he voyaged, the happier he became, though not, according to Nora, without assistance from drugs.

At Acapulco, to comply with a deal Errol had made with Columbia Pictures, the *Zaca* was rented for the shooting of sequences used in *The Lady from Shanghai.* The layover in port was lengthy, and Nora stayed for two weeks, enjoying the company of Orson Welles and Rita Hayworth, who were at that time married to each other. A doctor had examined Nora, and as the Flynn baby was safe, there existed no urgency to get back.

With biological discoveries made among the Mexican islands, Professor Flynn and Professor Hubbs also returned to Los Angeles. Errol's father, however, had made not only biological discoveries. *Errol and Me* relates that he had also found out about his son's drug-usage, and Errol accused Nora of making the revelation. In the midst of an argument, he hit her in the stomach with his knee, causing internal bleeding.

Whether she left the *Zaca* because of this incident or because of the pregnancy or because of Decker (or for all three reasons) is far from clear. She had ample reasons not to continue.

With these departures, the plans for the voyage changed. Errol revised his original destination and set sail for Cocos Islands. Having journeyed through the Panama Canal, the *Zaca* entered the Caribbean. For four days, by Errol's account, they were on the edge of a hurricane, and the wind, which he calculated at between ninety and a hundred miles per hour, ripped away the storm-sail. It took two men on the wheel to hold the *Zaca.* When they found a safe haven, it turned out to be Kingston, Jamaica.

For Errol, the place looked like paradise. He was never to keep his resolve to sail the *Zaca* to the South Seas, and her home-port for much of her life was to be Port Antonio, Jamaica. Errol vowed to return to the island, buy property and settle.

"After thirty-seven years of wandering," he declared, "I had found my Grecian isle."

Absence from Hollywood did not mean that Errol had entirely turned his back on moviemaking, because during the voyage he made two documentary films. One, *Deep Sea Fishing,* shot at Acapulco, was a slight affair lasting ten minutes. It showed Flynn and his archer-friend, Howard Hill, who had taught him how to use a bow for *Robin Hood,* fishing for marlin from a launch. Predictably, Hill used bow and arrow to impale marine life.

The other picture, at twice the length, was more ambitious and was appropriately called *The Cruise of the Zaca,* though it could be argued that this was a slight misnomer since Errol actually completed it in Jamaica, several intervals elapsing, well after the voyage had ended. It was shot in 16mm and colour.

He made one feature film only in 1946, a somewhat vapid comedy, *Never Say Goodbye,* perhaps chiefly notable because the man who "wasn't much of a parent" again performed attractively in his scenes with a juvenile, this time Patti Brady. But though Errol seemed lighthearted on screen, David Niven, having returned to Hollywood, found him changed – bitter and withdrawn. Niven noted the addiction to vodka, which Errol was then drinking mixed with 7-Up while in make-up at seven in the morning. He also observed that one of Errol's greatest buddies was still Bruce Cabot, a worthy drinking-companion but never a man to pick up the tab. Years later, when the Flynn finances foundered, Cabot was to inspire Errol to near-homicidal rage by unscrupulously trying to get money out of him.

In that same year, 1946, Errol also published his novel *Showdown.*

He had long been interested and showed facility in writing, and money and fame, at this stage in his life, were not the spurs that drove him to publish *Showdown.* Earlier in his life, he had kept notebooks and written for the *Bulletin,* Australia's most famous weekly at the time he was a contributor. Of *Beam Ends* (1937), his deft and entertaining – if also very slight – account of sailing up the east coast of Australia in 1930, Errol wrote, "It answered a need in myself."

When he became famous, he published articles in a number of magazines, and he once said, "I admired the writers around Hollywood more than I did the actors." This admiration was the expression of a wistful longing to develop what earlier choices and a disinclination to work had already deprived him of. In the psychological slump after the rape-trial, he came to terms, if only briefly, with his literary yearnings: "It dawned on me now that I was beaten as a writer too. That dream had been shattered. I had chosen to be an actor, to make big money, to become famous" – at the expense of his potential as an author. Nevertheless, he persisted, and the results included *Showdown* and *My Wicked, Wicked Ways,* the second – by any reckoning – a special case that will be discussed in detail in a later section of this book.

Showdown is a lengthy and ambitious novel, though its story is relatively simple. It concerns one Shamus O'Thames [*sic*]*, who agrees to pilot the tramp ship *Maski* and a Hollywood movie-company to the Sepik River. A shipwreck strands them on the New Guinea shore, and Shamus, trying to forget Ganice, his unattainable love, comes to see the worth of the lovely star of the company, Cleo Charnel [*sic*], as they are involved in dangerous adventures and a struggle for survival.

The tale is not quite so rudimentary as it sounds, and at one point, interestingly enough, it looks to be shaping up as Errol's parable of sacred and profane love, with Sister Ganice and Cleo as antithetical twins. However, the author abandons or at least fails to do justice to this theme. Even so, the two

*Probably named, however outlandishly, for a Flynn uncle – Oscar O'Thames.

strands to his narrative reveal something about the Flynn who could both advertise his conquests and, almost in the same breath, speak of platonic relationships with women.

Shamus first sees Sister Ganice in the midst of delirium brought on by blackwater-fever, and he observes that the "violet-grey eyes, the smooth high forehead, the lips even, might be his mother's. But why would his mother be wearing a starched white hood?" The "great priest" Father Kirshner tells Shamus, "She's young. She's as innocent and pure as a freshly opened flower." Clearly, Shamus must respect her religious vows, and so he resigns himself to unrequited love.

But along comes Cleo to make events take a healthier turn. She is dressed in "a pair of tight-fitting, deceiving blue jeans". ("Tight-fitting" *and* "deceiving"? Errol should have known better.) "Leaning elegantly upon the rail," she begins to work her magic upon him. At first, he sees her as vulgar and brash – Hollywood at its worst. Later, under stress, she reveals the fine, enduring qualities of a vibrant, sensuous woman. There is a well-written, semi-erotic sequence in which she and Shamus go swimming together in the nude: "As clear as in a lighted mirror, the moon revealed the full outline of her body, shimmering and incandescent, divine in the rippled wavelets beneath the surface."

This inversion in the personality of Cleo, counterpointed by similar inversions in other characters whom the callow Shamus has at first morally despised, is one of the best features of an unequal novel. The rest is conventional derring-do and plenty of local colour.

How high was Errol reaching?

It is hard to be certain, but *Showdown,* for all its philosophical and autobiographical overtones, is essentially an adventure-story, and a mediocre one, at that. The prose is careful, for the most part grammatical, and pedestrian. Although any page picked at random may reveal genuine talent, this long novel has an overall ordinariness that only a fanatical Flynn admirer would deny. To be blunt, it is Errol the man and actor who makes one endure Errol the novelist.

Once again, this area of his life displays both an undeveloped gift and a lack of self-discipline: had Errol possessed greater talents or had he pruned and rearranged his material to greater dramatic effect, the book would have been much better. As it is, this legacy of his literary aspirations is a long, hard slog for the reader.

Finally, taking the most generous view possible, one might be forgiven for suspecting that the author harboured the sneaking feeling that the name Errol Flynn on its covers might compensate for the inadequacies of any book he wrote.

That summer, in a characteristic episode before the cruise of the *Zaca,* Errol had encountered another sailor and actor, Sterling Hayden, at Newport Beach. In *Wanderer* – a remarkable book, profound and eloquent enough to make professional writers sigh with envy – Hayden described their meeting.

He was scraping varnish on his schooner *Quest* when Errol came sauntering down the dock wearing a beat-up yachting cap. Not unexpectedly, he had an attractive girl in tow, impeccably dressed in a new yachting outfit. Later, Hayden discovered that the girl, of whose name, even, Errol was not sure, had been a car-hop at an El Segundo drive-in until Flynn had picked her up the day before. She did not contribute to the conversation, and Errol spoke lightly of helping her in her showbiz ambitions.

As soon as Errol appeared, Hayden had recognized him, although the two had not met before. With what seriousness it is hard to gauge, Flynn suggested that Hayden might one afternoon come out on the *Zaca* to give him a sailing-lesson, but it was to his credit if he sincerely believed he had much to learn from the other man, since Hayden's experience dwarfed his own.

Hayden told him, "I first heard about you in Port Moresby, New Guinea, from a guy named MacKenzie who had a recruiting schooner. He said you owed him money."

"He's a bloody liar," Errol answered. "The truth of the matter is, I had a, shall we say, 'social disease' at the time. After I left, it seems his wife came down with it."

On Hayden's boat, the two actors talked for hours, sustaining themselves on vodka and scotch. The girl crawled into a bunk and slept, but when she later stirred, Errol casually pulled down the zipper of her slacks and erotically fondled his semi-anonymous companion. As they left, he promised to ditch her on the *Zaca* and return for Hayden so that they could hunt girls together at a place on Laguna Beach.

He did not return, and Hayden did not expect him to.

A second daughter, Rory, was born to Errol and Nora in March of 1947. The event caused him to take another look at their so-called marriage, the result of which was Errol's invitation that Nora should come to live permanently at Mulholland with him, and she did actually move in for about a year, a nursery having been built on to the house. However, he had waited too long, and there was now another man, whom she wanted to marry.

Before moving in to Mulholland, she made stipulations: Errol was not to bring other women to the house or to the *Zaca.* She knew the futility of insisting that he should stop seeing them elsewhere. However, on at least two occasions, she detected him in transgression of the rules. On the *Zaca* he entertained the leading lady of one of his films, and there was an occasion when a friend, not realizing Nora would be there, brought to Mulholland a girl Errol had picked up in Jamaica. Ironically, Nora recognized her, because she had spotted her in footage Errol shot for *The Cruise of the Zaca.*

If there was such a thing as casual trouble, Errol had by this time become an expert in it. Two examples taken from this period will show the sort of incident that was punctuating his life. One night after he and Nora had divorced, his lawyer called him to say that she wanted custody of both children. Full of rage and loaded with vodka, Errol stormed out to his car, which he backed out only to feel a wheel pass over something. When he got out to look, he discovered that he had fatally crushed his pet dachshund puppy, Grena.

Earlier, he had had a nasty run-in with the law. It started unspectacularly enough, if somewhat discourteously. In the company of a Warner Brothers public-relations man, Errol was on his way to a formal occasion in Manhattan. A police-car moved up alongside their taxi, and one of its two occupants told them to pull over to the kerb so that Errol could sign an autograph-book. In a hurry and with their composure rattled, the star and his companion protested with some warmth. Errol said, "Jesus, you made us pull over here and practically at gunpoint. Hitler wouldn't do this." At that, the cops took them to the station-house, where Errol, after a shove in the back, finally lost what was left of his temper, and a fight began. Errol came out of it badly. He recovered in a cell, in which he spent most of the night, and the affair was finally settled in the morning when he was fined fifty dollars for disturbing the peace. The injustice rankled, to say nothing of what the episode did to embitter Errol's attitude to the New York police.

Of course, fights dotted the entire course of his life. Those in which he was not the prime mover were often thrust upon him in public places such as bars by drunks and loudmouths, eager to prove that "that sonofabitch Flynn" wasn't so tough, after all. In fairness to the star, it has to be said that he became mortally weary of such confrontations, especially when their public settings provoked press-coverage, as they usually did. Like anybody else, Errol won some and lost some.

He was reported to have knocked out, among others, a stand-in and, at a party, an interior decorator. On the other hand, at a party given by Sonja Henie, Errol was knocked down by a millionaire called Dan Topping, of whom he said with typical aplomb, "There's no one I'd rather be hit by." Duncan McMartin, a prominent Canadian goldminer, tangled with Flynn in a bar in Nassau. Also widely reported was a fight in 1938 with Aidan Roark, the polo-player. Errol allegedly beat up a sea-captain on 9th August 1939. In both of these brawls, Flynn fared spectacularly well.

One of the most publicized brawls concerned Errol's dog Arno, the movie-columnist Jimmy Fidler and Mrs Fidler. After Arno, who was almost as famous as his master, had been lost overboard while the *Sirocco* was at sea, the Coast Guard called Errol to say that they had identified the dog's body by its collar. Perhaps Mr Flynn would like to claim the body. no, said Errol – not the body, but they could send him the collar.

He could not face looking at the dead Arno.

Hearing of the incident, Fidler made his own interpretation in print: that Errol, having exploited as publicity his love for the dog, cared so little in fact that he could not be bothered to claim the body.

(The accusation was patently unjust. Picture after picture, taken by amateurs as well as professionals, revealed that Errol's affection for Arno was just as warm and demonstrative whether he was aware of a lens in the vicinity or not.)

Shortly afterwards, star and columnist met by chance in a nightclub. Seeing Errol approach his table, Fidler held out his hand in greeting, but Errol clouted him so hard that the man toppled over on to the dance-floor. It was a qualified victory only, because while he was thinking over the next move, Mrs Fidler jabbed Errol in the ear with a fork. The matter was settled in court, where Errol quipped: "The lady obviously has good table manners. She used the right fork." Several big stars were present and watched the fight – among them Lupe Velez, reportedly brandishing a ketchup-bottle, and yelling, "Geev it to heem, beeg boy!" The "beeg boy" was presumably Errol Flynn.

His films continued to appear. An Errol improbably bespectacled appeared in *Cry Wolf,* the first of two films directed by Peter Godfrey, the Englishman who had formerly acted and produced in his own country. *Cry Wolf* was – for Flynn – an unusual picture but not a good one, though it had its effective moments. Despite a deliberately ambiguous aura in the early reels that could have signified villainy, Errol was the quiet, strong centre of this melodrama, and his next role, as a gifted composer, was also outside his customary range.

Escape Me Never had actually been completed in early 1946, but its release, for reasons that are not clear, was delayed for nearly two years. *The Constant Nymph,* also originally planned for Errol, had been made a few years before, with Charles Boyer, and both stories, with much in common, had been written by Margaret Kennedy. The plot and characters were little more convincing than those of *Cry Wolf,* but *Escape Me Never* had at least one claim to distinction – the last score, and a beautiful one at that, written for a Flynn

Errol, Alan Hale and Vincent Sherman on the set of *The Adventures of Don Juan*

Errol and Princess Irene Ghika – Royal Film Performance, 1949 (*That Forsyte Woman*)

During the making of *Montana*: Alexis Smith and Errol share a good joke

Errol and Patrice Wymore

Errol and Patrice with Deirdre, Rory and Arnella

Beverley Aadland – 'Woodsie'

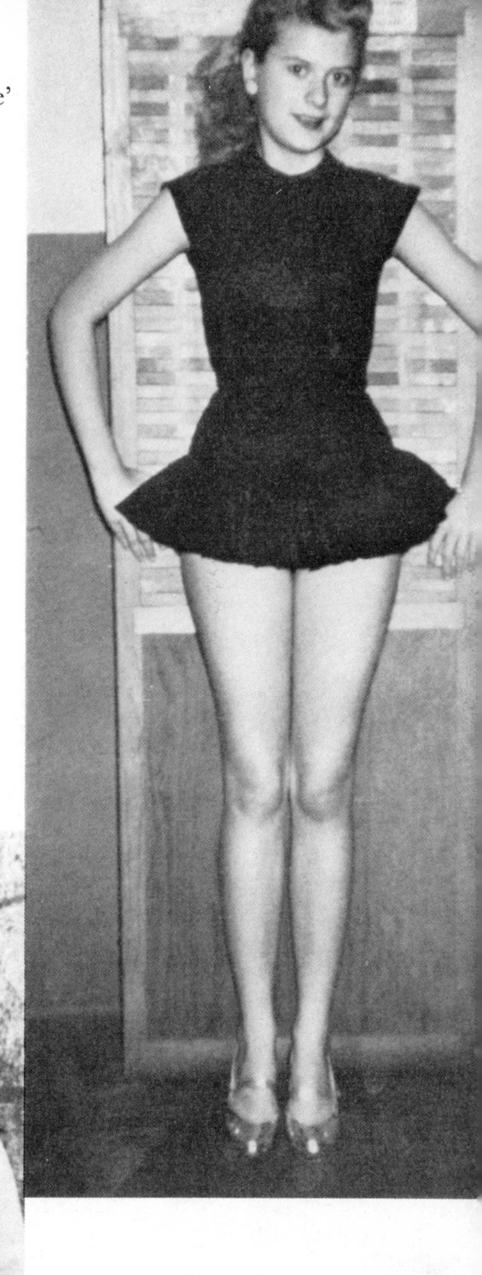

Sean Flynn as he appeared in *Duel on the Rio Grande*

The Sun Also Rises: Errol with Eddie Albert

The world's worst husband nurses a child in Africa

Errol during the making of *Cuban Rebel Girls*

Errol studies a painting: he backed John Decker's gallery and himself owned a Van Gogh and a Gauguin

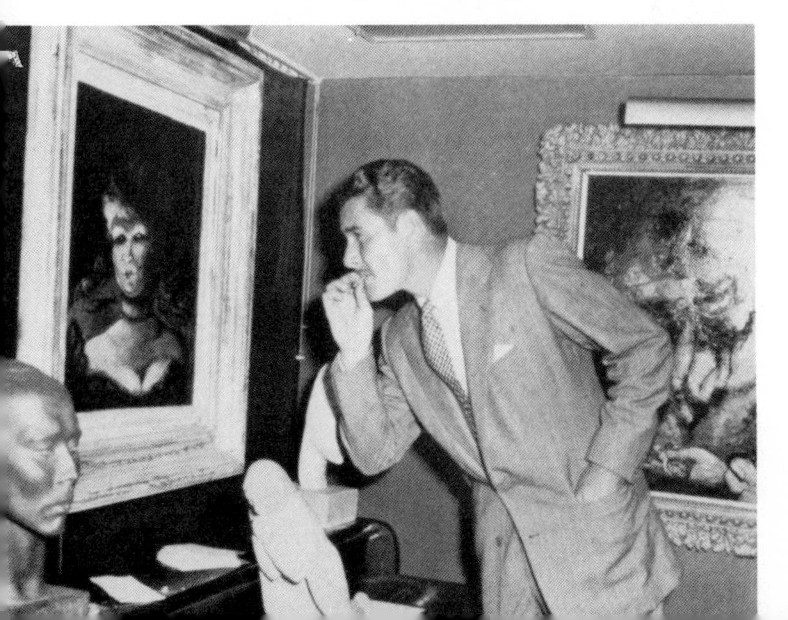

Fooling to the end: Errol and Eddie Albert relax during the making of *The Roots of Heaven*

picture by Erich Wolfgang Korngold.

Between Korngold and Steiner, with occasional interludes by composers such as Franz Waxman, Errol was extraordinarily lucky in the musical aspects of his pictures, and it was Max Steiner, yet again, who provided a powerful ingredient in the otherwise mediocre *Silver River* (1948), Errol's last production with 'Uncle' Raoul Walsh. After the split with Curtiz, who had the reputation of driving actors hard, Walsh had directed most of the best Flynn action-pictures, starting with *They Died With Their Boots On.*

But Errol was becoming tougher to control, more difficult to involve – a discovery Vincent Sherman was to make the hard way on *The Adventures of Don Juan* (1949), though it was possibly the best picture Errol had made since his first with Walsh. Even though the star's looks now showed clear signs of deterioration, Errol gave a splendid performance, perhaps aided by the self-mocking qualities of a script by George Oppenheimer and Harry Kurnitz. The action was magnificently handled, and the obligatory duel at the climax – this time, with a memorably nasty Robert Douglas – was once more staged by Fred Cavens. Max Steiner contributed one of his finest scores, and the commercial notion – to exploit the resemblance between the Don's amours and Errol's offscreen affairs – was softened by the style and humour.

In the final cut, audiences saw something like – strikingly like – the old Errol Flynn.

What they did not see was the star's on-set behaviour. Owing to drink, his playing was uncertain, creating problems, and these, combined with his lateness or non-appearance, inflated the budget to over two million dollars. The returns from US cinemas did not match the excellent ones in Europe, and Warner Brothers, as a result, substantially reduced the budgets of Errol's remaining films.

There was a greater cost to Errol, but it was one in which he wearily acquiesced: *Don Juan* turned its star into even more of a public joke than he had been before.

Sans dialogue, Errol appeared in the closing shots of *It's a Great Feeling* – a comic guest-shot; and in the same year, 1949, he played his first 'straight' role* in a 'straight' picture, Soames Forsyte in *That Forsyte Woman,* an adaptation of part of Galsworthy's *The Forsyte Saga.* His latest contract with Warners permitted him to make one loan-out film per year, and for this one he moved over to MGM.

That Forsyte Woman provided an absorbing interlude not only in Errol's film-career but also in his social life.

When the picture was selected for the Royal Film Performance in London, he turned up accompanied by Princess Irene Ghika, to whom he became engaged for a while soon after the break-up of his marriage to Nora. They had met in Paris, and the princess was about twenty – a member of the old ruling family of Rumania. She was attractive and very slim.

Although she came with Errol to London and visited his estate in Jamaica, the association lasted merely a few months. He said, "She just got tired of my ways and turned me down."

But Errol had probably never been too serious about the matter in the first place. The decision to end his marriage had been Nora's, not his, and his engagement to Princess Ghika seemed to be mainly a way of boosting his ego. To be seen with minor royalty on a royal occasion, for example, no doubt had its attractions.

But what of the film *That Forsyte Woman*?

It was not a very good picture, but Errol was good in it. The screenplay and treatment made Soames Forsyte seem even less attractive than Galsworthy had depicted him in his novels, but the Flynn charisma (to borrow a vogue-word from a later decade) turned him into a sympathetic character whose motives, if not commendable, were at least understandable. Errol had the extraordinary power – independent of acting, good or bad – of compelling audiences to identify with him, so that even when his on-screen conduct was questionable or downright bad, they still wanted him to succeed. Even so, charisma apart, his performance indicated that he had considerably more to offer in better, more substantial

*A debatable assertion, the author admits: Bette Davis, among others, has commented that Flynn gave a fine straight performance in *The Sisters.*

screenplays. However, the time was fast approaching when producers would not be interested either in graceful, romantic Errol or the latent, unexplored talents of actor Flynn.

Nora finally divorced Errol and married singer Dick Haymes soon afterwards.

In *My Wicked, Wicked Ways,* Errol wrote little of Nora between the bare announcement of his marriage to her in 1945 and the equally bare statement of their divorce in 1949.

Why did he marry her?

Whatever his feelings about her, it is arguable that he would never have done so if she had not become pregnant. After the rape-trial, the pressure put on their star by Warner Brothers can be imagined. He would have known that he must toe the line, that one more scandal would gravely imperil the career he had already jeopardized so recklessly. That he and Nora should legitimize their relationship was desirable, if not actually urgent.

Furthermore, there was the child, Deirdre, and Errol's claim to her. Poor father and hopeless husband that he was, Errol, when it came to divorce, wanted the custody of *both* children – an unrealistic wish that at any rate illustrated his feelings for his progeny.

Nora had had much to put up with. Nearly twenty years his junior, she had married a man infinitely old in his vices. Even though they lived apart for most of the time, she suffered the brutality of his drug-induced rages as well as his constant infidelities. Twice, she had attempted suicide.

For his part, Errol had tried, after the birth of Rory, to be a husband and father – had at least begged for the chance. "I was beginning," he explained pathetically, "to think of the children more than of myself and more than of Nora, but I was too late."

Warner Brothers made their economies in the budgets for Flynn pictures, and two Westerns, neither distinguished, came out in 1950. *Montana* contained little that was memorable, but in a statistical sense, *Rocky Mountain* was exceptional in two ways: it was the last Flynn Western and the film on which he met the "attractive, warm, wholesome" Patrice Wymore. He once said of Patrice: "Gradually I found she was the complete antithesis of everything I had looked for in a woman. I expected vanity. She had none. I expected lies. It took me five years to catch her out in one. I was used to feminine wiles. She never thought of them. I'd find it amusing when dolls tried to sell me a bill of goods. She didn't try to sell anything . . . No tricks. Just directness, sincerity and the kind of forthrightness that is not capable of being shaken by criticism. I found something to respect."

To understand his third and last marriage, one has to realize that Errol Flynn was at this point like a man trying hard to grab a rope that was paying out too fast for him. He knew that he was losing any fight that he might have been putting up against his addictions. He had become a notorious legend and a public buffoon. He knew that his great days as a star were over.

This time, he really hoped and perhaps even believed that marriage might save him as a human being, confer the stability that had so far eluded him. But from the outset he was aware of the problems. Patrice Wymore was nearly twenty years his junior, and Errol might have been described as old for his age. To some extent he was *inventing* a role for her without consulting her – that of *Hausfrau* – and he was alive to the falsity of what he was doing.

It was obvious what Errol saw in Patrice.

But what did she see in him?

When he himself asked her that question, her reply was that she felt sorry for him. As a basis on which to wed, it was fairly realistic, and the answer was enough for the 'new' Errol Flynn.

After a civil ceremony in Monte Carlo, they were married on 23rd October 1950, at the French Lutheran Church of the Transfiguration in Nice – in marked contrast to his previous private, almost furtive, wedding-ceremonies. Patrice was twenty-four, and Errol was forty-one. Outside the church, there were hundreds (Errol claimed three thousand) of people, and the reception at the Hôtel de Paris was no vicarage tea-party. In the midst of it, one of Errol's guests took him aside to inform him that a man at the door had a warrant for the actor's arrest.

Ever the practical joker himself, Errol suspected that he was the prospective victim of a gag.

But this was no gag.

The document charged that on board the *Zaca* a year before Errol Flynn had raped a seventeen-year-old, Denise Duvivier.

A stunning start to married life.

A stunning setting for the alleged crime – the very boat Errol had purchased to free himself of memories inspired by the *Sirocco*.

A nightmare seemed to be repeating itself, but Errol, who recalled no Denise Duvivier, decided to answer the charge as he was required to, in the Monaco town hall. A journalist-friend advised against this course of action; there was no bail in Monaco. However, almost as a moral protest, Errol made up his mind to go through with it.

He broke the news to his wife, and, the reception over, they returned to the *Zaca* for their wedding-night. In the morning, they were roused by guns and rockets fired by ships of the American navy, which had surrounded the *Zaca* at Villefranche, presumably while the couple slept. Well-intentioned sailors, full of congratulations for their idol, even disturbed what should have been a tranquil meal in a waterfront restaurant. In his haste to escape their attentions, Errol leapt into their launch, slipped and passed out cold from the resultant pain.

The introvert within the extrovert had paid the price again. He wrote, "No one ever believe[d] I want[ed] some peace, quiet, the soft moments of life." This time, the price of attempted privacy had come high. His third, fourth and fifth lumbar vertebrae were fractured, and he was to be flat on his back for a month.

When he had recovered, he and Patrice sailed to Monte Carlo harbour, an action for which he had these words: "Returning to Monaco was the only brave thing I ever did in my life."

Monacan law required that an accusing party should

confront the accused in the presence of a magistrate. Errol already had some idea of what – or whom – to expect, since French newspapers had printed a picture showing him and Denise Duvivier, fully clothed, apparently embracing at the rail of the *Zaca.* The picture was not a fake, but the circumstances in which it had been taken were a mystery to Errol, especially since he did not recognize the girl.

What Patrice, his bride, was thinking has not been recorded, but she was certainly behaving like the ally and support her husband had hoped for.

At the hearing, the magistrate listened impassively to Errol's denial of the charge. Then La Duvivier was brought in. Seeing pigtails yet again, Errol was sickened by memories of California and the earlier accusations. But the rest of what he saw convinced him that he could never have made love to this girl.

Especially in the shower on his yacht.

Such was the allegation.

Errol could have expatiated on the problems of rape in such confined quarters – in his own words, "an upright coffin". Instead, controlling himself with an effort, he invited the judge to visit the *Zaca* and inspect the supposed scene of the supposed crime.

Result: case dismissed.

Tragedy, or the threat of it, had been turned into farce. Perhaps Errol would have chosen neither, but he was reasonably happy about the outcome, and the French public were joyful. Though the nature of his popularity might not have been to his taste, he had evidence that it still existed on a large scale.

There was a postlude – the solution to the mystery of the photograph taken about a year earlier. The girl had swum out to the *Zaca,* climbed aboard and stumbled against Errol so that he involuntarily caught her. Among the sightseers and visitors who thronged about the yacht, one of those with a camera had been waiting for precisely this moment.

The whole sequence of events proved, if it proved anything, that Errol was now fair game for this sort of thing.

As his career ran down, Errol was not alone, in the sense that Hollywood and its workers were in a turmoil – not to say panic – at the impact of television on the industry. Economies were called for, and heads began to roll – often those of the stars themselves, since their services were the most costly. That might have been small consolation to Errol, but he found greater comfort in Patrice, to whom he later paid tribute for her steadfastness. For a while they were happy, though she made the same discoveries about him that his previous wives had made and, of the three women, possibly knew him at his lowest psychological point.

Errol's gaiety, Patrice found, was often at that time a mask for desperation, though the prankster was still in him. He was a man's man, even if he leaned on her as perhaps he had not done on Lili and Nora. Significantly, his marriage was to falter with the revival of his career, and he afterwards wrote: "I tried to stay interested in my wife but that was hard. It is hard for me to stay interested in any one woman in the world for very long, no matter how fine she is."

In 1951, he made *Kim,* some of which was shot in India. Wanting to visit India, Errol made a bad choice or was poorly advised. He turned down the lead in MGM's *King Solomon's Mines,* which was enormously successful and greatly aided Stewart Granger's career. However, perhaps too much should not be made of this unfortunate decision: the lives of actors are full of such 'might-have-beens'. However, local colour did not make the dramatic proceedings any less lethargic, though Errol, in red beard and turban, looked handsome. Despite top billing, he played second fiddle to Dean Stockwell as he had to the Mauch twins in *The Prince and the Pauper.* That same year, Errol appeared in the curiosity *Hello, God,* a semi-allegorical and rarely shown picture whose release he eventually tried to block.

The third picture of 1951 was a nautical adventure-story called *The Adventures of Captain Fabian,* which was produced and directed by William Marshall, who was responsible for the same functions (plus writing and narration) on *Hello, God. Captain Fabian* was a protracted (100 minutes) bore, the more dismal for the fact that Errol himself had written the limp screenplay – as lacking in lustre as the leading man's own eyes, the missing sparkle of which seemed to be the chief casualty of his dissipation.

Mara Maru (1952) was almost as leaden, with the star looking more and more tired, as he did, too, in the same year's *Against All Flags,* a milk-and-water swashbuckler.

Then, after a first-class row with Jack Warner, he split with Warner Brothers.

No matter how sour the ending or how shabby the handling of the star's vehicles in the later years, the studio had served Errol Flynn well. As an illustration, merely consider his co-actors: de Havilland (eight pictures), Ann Sheridan (three), Alexis Smith (three), Rathbone (three), Claude Rains (three), and such varied talents as Paul Kelly, Alan Hale, Victor Francen, Patric Knowles, Ian Hunter and David Niven.

Not that Errol had not merited and repaid the care put into his films. He had proved himself as formidable a scene-stealer as any of the actors listed above. He had worked hard or had been made to work hard for Michael Curtiz and Raoul Walsh. Within his limitations or those imposed on him by the studio, he had performed admirably.

He had scaled the heights of success and fame. He had also plumbed the depths of notoriety and scandal.

Now he began to know the bitterest taste of failure, not least financial failure.

9

Desperate Journey

In a fifty-fifty partnership with Italians, Errol had had plans to film *William Tell* in Italy. He wrote the outline himself and would also play Tell. This historical epic was to be the first CinemaScope feature and was budgeted for $860,000, Errol providing half with his own cash.

Disaster came quickly and completely.

In June 1953, exteriors were shot in Northern Italy by the director Jack Cardiff, but the Italian backers soon faded, and it became clear that the principal one had put up only *half* his agreed share. There were other questionable angles, but the basic financial picture was clear – and bleak. As if the blow that had fallen were not enough, Al Blum, Errol's business manager, died, and Errol discovered that he owed the US Government $840,000 in back taxes.

To put it conservatively, Blum had not been a good manager. To put it more bluntly, he had misappropriated funds, using them for his own gambling. As Errol expressed it, Al Blum "had only taken care of himself". At least Blum died penitent, some of his last words being: "Tell Errol I am sorry."

While he was still staggering from the shock of *William Tell's* inevitable shutdown, Errol's friend Bruce Cabot had two process-servers in Rome seize Errol's two cars and Patrice's clothes. Cabot, who had been working on *Tell,* had hoped to get some money out of Errol rather than sue the Italian backers.

To complete the holocaust, Lili Damita, according to Errol, had during this period tied up everything she could lay her hands on in Hollywood belonging to her ex-husband – for back alimony. The assets included his house and furniture.

The blows had come thick and fast, and if Errol did not go under, he certainly reeled from them.

For four years between 1952 and 1956, he spent much of the time cruising the Mediterranean in the *Zaca.* The days of wandering – Naples, Rome, Palma de Majorca, Jamaica – had begun with a vengeance, and he was embarked also on a succession of the worst films he ever made.

But he did not whine during this dismal spell, though he sought the traditional solace of the bottle. He tried to pay off his debts and rebuild his life.

He had Patrice, but he had lost his star-status, he was to lose his cash-assets, and he had spoiled the acting-asset of phenomenal good-looks. He was drinking purposefully, and though he denied the fact, he was fairly certainly hooked on drugs. The area of doubt lay in the degree of dependence.

In *My Wicked, Wicked Ways,* Errol wrote: "I have taken many and most drugs, but I am not an addict. The only drug I have never taken is heroin. Take it once, you are hooked, done for. So it is not for me." Brave words. But they were being recorded at a time when Errol, unaware of his imminent death, still had some regard for his reputation and the harm as well as the good his autobiography might do him. Furthermore, Nora Eddington has pointed out that, like so many addicts and alcoholics, Errol believed he could master his habits, quit when he wanted to.

Salvaging what he could from his pay-cheques, he had used the money to enlarge the Errol Flynn Estates in Jamaica.

Jamaica was his haven – his secret world. So far away from Hollywood, he managed during his visits to lead a secluded life – secluded at least from gossip-columnists and prying journalists, many of whom were not even aware that he owned Boston Estate on the island. If one reads between the lines, Errol was in another sense the very centre of an attention he welcomed; for to the Jamaican people, whose courtesy and naturalness he loved, Flynn was a king.

He described Jamaica as "an incessant rolling and unravelling hill" and enjoyed its beautiful landscape as much as he enjoyed the charm of its inhabitants. On his visits, he would land at Kingston airport, hire a limousine and have himself driven across the island to the estate, its boundary marked by a blue fence about two miles long with occasional signs proclaiming: Errol Flynn Estates. There he enjoyed swimming, walking, horseback-riding – and fleeting tranquillity.

But if Errol had a haven in his life, he was not one, even in his later years, to spend his life in a haven.

Jamaica was his retreat, his temporary refuge, but he never did settle there in the real meaning of the word, and all the signs were that he never would have done. Nearly eight years after his death, Errol's fondness for Jamaica had an interesting legal sequel. Mr Justice Megarry, a London High Court Judge, had to decide where Flynn spent most of his life. He rejected the submission that the actor's legal home had been New York, California or Tasmania and said that he thought the island was the most enduring love of Flynn's life. The judge was ruling in a dispute over Errol's English estate between the two executors – his widow Patrice Wymore and the New York attorney Justin Morton Golenbock.

But Errol knew himself well enough to realize that he would never settle there – an awareness that found expression in an extract from his diary quoted near the end of *My Wicked, Wicked Ways:*

> *Boston Estate, Jamaica, 4th April 1954:*
> My dream of happiness. A quiet spot by the Jamaica seashore, looking out at the activity in the ocean, hearing the wind sob with the beauty and the tragedy of everything. Looking out over nine miles of ocean, hearing some happy laughter nearby; sitting under an almond tree, with the leaf spread over me like an umbrella, that is my dream of happiness.
> Unfortunately, an hour later, I might not be happy with that.

That last sentence tells all. From time to time, he found periods of happiness, all right.

But he was never to find peace – perhaps because he never really wanted it.

He surely failed to find it in Italy in the early 'fifties. Having had enough of Lili and her alimony, he had taken refuge there with Patrice – only to run into the *William Tell* fiasco.

But that year, 1953, was to end a little more happily with the birth of a daughter, Arnella, on Christmas Day in Rome.

Arnella was Errol's last child. Since his death, all four children have frequently been in the news. Arnella has acting ambitions. Rory became a model, and Deirdre has worked as stuntgirl, stand-in and actress. Without repeating his father's success, Sean starred in *The Son of Captain Blood.* Later, he went to Vietnam as a photographer for *Paris Match.* In 1970, he moved to Cambodia, and while attempting to shoot some of the action there, he disappeared and has been presumed dead, although his mother, Lili Damita, it is reported, has been trying to locate him.

Errol's account of those years is a kaleidoscope, by turns picaresque, wistful, glamorous and hedonistic: the jet-set in Rome; skin-diving off the coast of Spain; a nostalgic visit to England and the Northampton Repertory Company; a brawl on the *Zaca.*

Possibly the visit to Northampton – he called it a "sentimental journey" – was the highlight. When he spoke to an audience and told them he had spent the happiest days of his life there, they laughed, seemingly incredulous.

They could have been right. They could have been wrong.

But before fame and fortune, life *had* been happy – or at least simpler.

No wives, no alimony.

No agents, managers and deals.

And when a gun jammed in a play, you could walk to the footlights and tell the audience, "There is a slight hitch!" (Errol had done so all those years ago, when he was playing Bulldog Drummond.)

Life had been simpler.

In England, he made *The Master of Ballantrae* in 1953. It was surprisingly good, but the same could not be said for *Crossed Swords* (1954), filmed in Italy with a soporific screenplay and scant vigour in the direction.

There was little to be said, and most of it bad, about the two Herbert Wilcox productions of 1955 made in England, *Let's Make Up (Lilacs In The Spring)* and *King's Rhapsody.* Though the first did quite good business in its country of origin, the second expired at the box-office everywhere, though it may be remembered as the second and last picture in which Patrice Wymore appeared with her husband. (However, they did appear together on television. In 1956, Errol and Patrice returned to England to make a series of half-hour TV films, produced by Norman Williams and French-Canadian financier Marcel Leduc, who hoped the Errol Flynn Theatre would rival the Douglas Fairbanks Theatre. The series did moderately well, but no fortunes were made, and it was not extended.)

In *Let's Make Up,* Errol sang and danced ("Lily of Laguna") and proved that he could still be fascinating – not just a jaded star attempting what he should never have tried even in his younger days.

It was said that Herbert Wilcox had arranged to save Errol from his financial straits if Flynn would co-star with Anna Neagle in two films. But the teaming simply did not work in either artistic or commercial terms, and Wilcox was to admit that just as Neagle fans were not Flynn fans, so the reverse was true. Mention of Errol, incidentally, was conspicuously absent from Wilcox's memoirs.

The Warriors (The Dark Avenger) (1955) was the last Flynn swashbuckler and unexceptionable but not memorable entertainment, filmed on location in England. If, as he said he was, Errol was now too old and tired for this sort of vehicle, the genre itself was probably also temporarily played out, having reached a peak in 1952 with *Scaramouche* and the remake of *The Prisoner of Zenda,* in both of which Stewart Granger had shown himself a worthy rival to Flynn but in no sense his better.

Tired footsteps in the darkest period of an apparently washed-up career, Errol's films paid the rent though they did little else except depress him. But he was about to turn a corner with a production that, if no milestone of cinema itself, would stimulate interest in the semi-forgotten star.

Sam Jaffe, who now represented him, secured for Errol the lead in *Istanbul* (1956), which was a remake of the 1947 *Singapore,* with Fred MacMurray and Ava Gardner. *Istanbul* was poor stuff, and Errol looked desperately tired in it. His voice, once so vital and fresh, had utterly lost its alluring timbre. Much to the star's disgust, since he had hoped to sail there from Majorca on the *Zaca,* the eponymous Istanbul, save for a few establishing shots, turned out to be the Universal back-lot, but *The Big Boodle* (1957) at least had genuine location-work and a dogged but again fatigued performance from Errol. The picture was filmed in Havana, with considerable footage of action in and around the famous Morro Castle.

However, it was Darryl Zanuck's production of *The Sun Also Rises* (1957) that really made both audiences and critics sit up to take another look at the ageing Flynn, so different from the one they knew of old. As Mike Campbell (who, in one of the few jokes Ernest Hemingway ever made, went bankrupt two ways – "suddenly and gradually"), Errol displayed to perfection the surface urbanity of a personality that could suddenly erupt into savage frustration and despair, as in a café-sequence in which he overturns without warning a table at which he is sitting. Stolidly directed by Henry King, *The Sun Also Rises* was a film of considerable longueurs, but Errol was magnificent in his aura of fatigue and tragedy. Characteristically, he shrugged off praise with a flippant attempt at deception – "Why all the fuss? After all, I just played myself." It would have been truer to say that he had found within himself the emotional sources for an unusually fine performance. In this psychological terrain, he looked like a seasoned traveller, and he was: he had been there.

The film had one aspect of defeat for Errol, however. He struggled against what was a huge demotion for him, but he had to accept fourth billing.

Several years earlier, Henry King had directed another and much better adaptation from Hemingway for the same studio (Fox), *The Snows of Kilimanjaro.* (It was written by Casey Robinson, oddly enough, the fine scriptwriter who had created the screenplay of *Captain Blood.*) It is interesting – if useless – to speculate how well Errol might have filled the role of Harry Street in *The Snows of Kilimanjaro,* even though Gregory Peck gave one of his finest performances in the part. The central character, with his long retrospective on a full but wasted existence, might have elicited from Flynn the performance of his life.

The screen career picked up, but ironically Errol was making his last two big pictures. If there was something lacking in his portrayal of John Barrymore in *Too Much, Too Soon* (1958), script deficiencies could be blamed rather than any in Errol's acting, and the smooth underplaying of his impersonation, deliberately avoiding direct imitation of the Barrymore he had known so well, represented an honest attempt to get inside the man. Certain stills from the production, it must be remarked, show an uncanny visual resemblance between Flynn and Barrymore that was not generally visible in the film, even though Errol had an extra 'blob' put on the end of his nose.

Having carried out his last obligation under the expired Warner Brothers contract with *The Master of Ballantrae,* Errol was back at his old studio for *Too Much, Too Soon.* If the ravages of time and dissipation on the features of the man who had created *Captain Blood* were obvious, they of course fitted the part he was playing. But Jack Warner had a different impression of the Errol he saw then. "He was," he said, "one of the living dead."

Yet not lacking in a quick interest.

While he was working on the picture in 1957, Errol met the fifteen-year-old Beverly Aadland, who was a dancer in the same studio's *Marjorie Morningstar* and with whom he was to spend a considerable amount of time in the last two years of his life. His pet-name for her was Woodsie, because she reminded him of a wood-nymph. He said that she amused him, and that, though oversimplified, might have been no more than the truth.

Errol was prematurely aged, and, drained and spent, he surely saw in her the vitality he had lost, the youth that he craved in what was left of his life. Had he been a different man in different circumstances, he might have found that youth in his own children. But he was not. He was Errol Flynn, who not long before in his own diary had listed his favourite occupation as "a prolonged bout in the bedroom".

Like Nora Eddington, Beverly Aadland stated that she was

a virgin when she met Errol and that compulsion was involved in their first love-making. Beverly was five and a half feet tall, blonde and with hazel eyes. In the manner of Peggy Satterlee, she was in the habit of lying consistently about her age in order to get work, and from the years of twelve or thirteen, she had usually passed for at least four or five years more than her real age. Since she soon became Errol's constant companion, her mother, Florence Aadland, customarily went with them to avert legal trouble. Beverly even travelled to Africa to join Errol when he was filming *The Roots of Heaven.*

On her seventeenth birthday, Errol announced their engagement (September 1959), and it was said that he would marry her just as soon as he could get a divorce from Patrice Wymore. To that end, his later plans to sell the *Zaca* were supposedly a way of raising money for a settlement. That rumour could have been true, but it was probably also convenient by then for a fatigued Errol to divest himself of the yacht.

In *Errol and Me,* Nora Eddington wrote that at the time he first associated with Beverly, there were tentative plans for Errol to play the lead in the film of Nabokov's *Lolita.* If he ever had done, it could truly have been said that art tended to imitate life.

At this stage in Errol's revived career, he did what perhaps seemed a strange thing: early in 1958, he agreed to take the lead in *The Master of Thornfield Hall,* an adaptation for the stage from *Jane Eyre,* written by his friend "the wealthy and cultured playboy", Huntington Hartford. There were try-outs in Detroit and Cincinnati, but Errol quit the play before it reached New York. In *My Wicked, Wicked Ways,* he asserted that the archaic language inhibited his performance.

His performance was inhibited, all right; but by the fact that he could not memorize his lines. He was past his prime, beyond heavy concentration, and a full-length play called for a feat of memory that was beyond the actor who could still learn the few lines of dialogue needed for any one day's shooting on a film.

(Beverly Aadland said after Errol's death that, although she did not know of the incident at the time, Patrice Wymore visited him while he was appearing in the play. The information is interesting, if only because so little seems to be known about Patrice during the later years. Gradually but definitely – and with a great deal of dignity, she had moved out of Errol's life as his career recovered. Coincidentally or by intention, she had stuck by him throughout the leanest period, and whatever else he did to her, he never forgot his debt to her. After they had parted, she, for her part, said: "I wish I could hate him, but I can't. He's the most lovable man in the world.")

In his autobiography, Errol's at best uncertain chronology lapsed yet again at this point in his life, and one of the results was that he neglected to mention a positive reason he had for walking out on *The Master of Thornfield Hall* – not that his negative reasons were not urgent enough. He had had another offer from Zanuck, this time to star – though in the event he had comparatively little to do – in John Huston's *The Roots of Heaven* (1958).

Filmed on location in French Equatorial Africa, this sadly inept picture made casualties of more than twenty of its crew. Errol recorded that "the medical problems ranged from a cut toe to amoebic dysentry, gonorrhea, malaria". One case of malaria was his own, though he did not succumb until after the company had returned to Paris.

As for his performance, it was yet another opportunity to use some of his own self on the screen – perhaps as Zanuck had intended it to be. Errol played a drunken ex-army-officer, and there was no denying the appeal of the man as it emerged in his jaded idealism, his *épuisé* air and his fatalistic courage. How much of it was acting in the sense of creating traits that he did not already possess might be debated, but the impression the actor made was a vivid one.

And not only in the picture itself.

Cynthia Grenier, who visited the unit while Huston was shooting at Fontainebleau, photographed what she saw and later wrote perceptively of her first glimpse of Errol *(Sight and Sound,* Autumn, 1958). He presented a disturbing appearance: "From about fifteen feet away Flynn looked the fine figure of a swashbuckler he was for many years on the screen. Up closer he still cut a pretty muscular figure for a man of forty-nine, but the face had a slightly disquieting aspect as if a thin layer of spongy tissue had been inserted between the skin and bone. An amiable, sardonic expression lit the face."

Errol had by that time been in hospital, partly because of his malaria-bout but also because of his back. He commented that it "acted up" from time to time. When Huston shot his death-scene for the picture, a toy poodle, presumably belonging to Beverly, was so convinced by his acting, that it rushed forward and tried to revive Errol by licking his face. Errol spoke firmly but kindly to reassure it. During Miss Grenier's visit, he was endearingly ironic, tired but urbane.

She left, however, with that significant first impression, the more haunting in retrospect.

Errol's achievements in *Too Much, Too Soon, The Roots of Heaven* and *The Sun Also Rises* were all the more remarkable because of the nature of the films, which were in no sense Flynn vehicles. At his peak, Warner Brothers had constructed pictures around him from screenplays that were tailormade to display his most obvious talents. Errol's supporting casts had been truly *supporting*: no matter how good the players, – and many of them were first-rate – they would have found it difficult if not impossible to steal the film from the star, if only because their parts were proportionately smaller than his. There had been exceptions, such as *The Prince and the Pauper,* but this was the general pattern.

Now professional life was different for Errol Flynn. In *The Sun Also Rises,* comparatively low down in the cast-list, he had to compete for attention with such players as Eddie Albert, Mel Ferrer and Tyrone Power – who, with a career not unlike Flynn's and after starting as a purveyor of charm and good-looks, had over the years become an experienced and considerable actor. In *The Roots of Heaven,* Errol again had the equally experienced Eddie Albert to reckon with, plus Trevor Howard, an idiosyncratic actor but not one without unusual power.

Errol had passed the point at which, even if he wanted to, he could rely upon rare handsomeness – though his looks, it must be admitted, carried their own ravaged authority. In such company and playing such unheroic or anti-heroic roles, he acquitted himself with a distinction that said much for the acting-style he had evolved over two decades. He had never studied. Until this time, he had never tried particularly hard. But he had worked with great directorial and histrionic talents, and all the time, perhaps despite himself, he had been learning.

In any case, not for nothing did a director like Raoul Walsh, even in his eighties, list Errol as one of the actors he liked best to work with. Whatever problems Errol had created through drinking or fighting the studio, he had been – when he wanted to be – the complete professional, ideally co-operative at bringing in a picture on schedule and within the budget.

With his charm depleted or damaged, he had experience to fall back on.

The Roots of Heaven really marked the end of Errol's life on the screen, but there was a shabby postlude. He went to Cuba to make *Cuban Rebel Girls* (1959), in which Beverly Aadland played the female lead. A veritable farrago, with muddled political views and technical inadequacies, the picture, a sure nomination for Flynn's worst, deserves only to be forgotten as a kindness, and Errol's motives in making it were opaque, though it has been suggested that it was produced as a tax write-off.

For a man of Errol's literary talents, an autobiography seemed both inevitable and desirable: with the most personal material of all to work on, he might at last triumph in an area where he had previously enjoyed only qualified success. But whether he knew it or not, he had left the task of writing it dangerously – and, as it turned out, impossibly – late.

Towards the end of 1958 G. P. Putnam's Sons of New York, having already made Errol an advance for a work that seemed unlikely to materialize, asked Earl Conrad to collaborate with the dilatory author to produce *My Wicked, Wicked Ways.* Conrad spent ten weeks at Boston Estate in Jamaica, where he interviewed Errol daily with two court stenographers in attendance to note all that was said. From these notes and adopting Errol's anecdotal and wry style, Conrad, taking the best part of a year, wrote the autobiography.

In retrospect, it is obvious that Errol needed money and that this need undoubtedly coloured some of his 'recollections' – perhaps even the whole tone of the book. The commercial possibilities of this highly commercial volume were enticing. Also with hindsight, it is clear that he was at that time too far gone with drink and drugs to do the work unaided. Earl Conrad did a highly professional job, and any weaknesses inherent in the autobiography, up to and including an astonishing disregard for facts, are attributable to Flynn rather than Conrad, who was scarcely in a position to check, for example, some of the Australian stories later revealed as bogus by John Hammond Moore and others.

My Wicked, Wicked Ways has a candour that is part genuine and in part a mask. For all its air of shocking revelations, the perceptive reader will discover little real 'wickedness' in it, and when he does, he will probably recognize one of Errol's fabrications or exaggerations. These 'lies', interestingly enough, are singularly self-revealing and provide a valuable index of the man's character. On the positive side, there are genuinely moving passages, as well as those displaying the abortive talent that its owner knew he had neglected in favour of easier, more lucrative occupations. His self-analysis, the autobiography shows, could be merciless, his insights acute – as when he says in one of his flashes of mordant perception, "I didn't know then that the congenital disease of America is that Americans buy success, and almost nothing else." (By the late 'fifties, he had learned that lesson the hard way.)

Even so, *My Wicked, Wicked Ways* leaves questions tantalizingly unanswered – and not just those about the strange omissions and confusions of its earlier sections. (John Hammond Moore's explanation that Errol's befuddled mind and penchant for tall stories had combined to blur the picture is as good as any other.) For example, why did he lavish mainly reticence on Nora Eddington? Why had he no real praise for Curtiz and Walsh and no praise at all for Korngold and Steiner? Why did he write so bitterly of Warner Brothers?

The answers are not hard to find.

Errol was counting his assets, not his debts – especially not his debts of gratitude. He must have felt some shame, too, about his behaviour towards Nora – more than he actually expresses in the book. He was acutely conscious of what he had not done rather than of the accomplishments that, some might have argued, were as much those of others as his alone. His bitterness towards Warner Brothers can readily be construed as his own displaced guilt-feelings about talents that could have been exploited to different effect but less commercially.

Above all, when he came to compose his autobiography, Errol had hardened, and he had jettisoned, along with sentimentality, some redeeming sentiment and compassion.

For all its flaws, *My Wicked, Wicked Ways* is required reading for anyone who wants to understand Errol Flynn. John Hutchens of the *New York Herald Tribune* was probably right when he wrote, "Throughout his bizarre life, as anyone can see, he was a rascal and frequently a fool. But those who rush to sit in judgment of him owe it to themselves to read him first."

Among those hurt by the publication of the autobiography were Professor and Mrs Flynn – not so much for anything their son had said about them as for the picture he had painted of himself. "Wicked" in the title worried them, but, then, Errol had clearly used the word ironically and satirically. As for their protests that he had been a good son and a courteous gentleman, that women had preyed on him, that he had been more than a playboy, they were all justified.

Justified, but incomplete.

If *My Wicked, Wicked Ways* does nothing else, it illustrates how many facets there were to Errol.

His parents talked of producing their own "sequel", which would be a corrective to the original, a recital of the virtues of their son.

But they never did. Marelle died in 1967, three weeks after

having been hit by a car in a street-accident, and Theodore died the following year.

In the summer of 1959, Errol visited Putnam's to correct the galleys of his book. He then went on to Hollywood, where his participation in a thirty-minute television picture, *The Golden Shanty,* was a harrowing experience for those who witnessed it. Once again, Errol had big trouble with his lines, but this time he could not even read the various prompt-cards that had been distributed about the set to help him.

His waning vitality might have been judged from his decision to sell the *Zaca,* which had symbolized so much for him. He and Beverly Aadland flew to Vancouver on 9th October to meet his friends Mr and Mrs George Caldough, who seemed likely to purchase the yacht. Errol had shown symptoms of exhaustion in Hollywood, and his back, perhaps as a result of the injuries sustained just after his third marriage, had been troubling him.

But the Canadian press was treated to at least a glimpse of the old Flynn when reporters interviewed him at Vancouver airport. True, his face was that of a tired man, but it had the inevitable moviestar tan, and there was an occasional twinkle in the eyes. He was thicker around the waist, naturally, but he was still a figure to command attention. The old, unregenerate, impudent spirit was in his quip: "I've always been one to burn the midnight Errol. Gentlemen, you may write that I intend to devote the rest of my life to litigation and women."

Predictably, he won the hearts of the reporters. If anything, his legendary charm had increased, so that it was impossible not to like the man. Here was no dissipated wreck, no incoherent alcoholic.

Were, then, the rumours of his decline and disintegration exaggerated?

Well, yes, of course they were.

But not that much.

Evidence about his drinking conflicted, but he was probably holding it down to a fifth of vodka a day. However, the words 'holding down' tell all.

And there was always the Flynn survival kit.

"I had a little kit that I carried around," he wrote. "It was about the size of a medical kit. On it were the words FLYNN ENTERPRISES. Only I knew that inside of it was a tidy bar, with a bottle of vodka, two or three glasses and a bottle or two of quinine water. I had acquired a bible at last and I carted it around with me."

Did he still have it?

By his own account, it had certainly been his constant companion in the early 'fifties and as late as 1956. As for his drug-usage, always hard to gauge, it might have tapered off. But nobody could be sure, and the questions were in a sense academic: too much damage had already been done.

While he and Beverly were still in Vancouver, Errol suffered severe back-pains, and when, with the deal for the *Zaca* all but settled, he was en route to the airport, the Caldoughs stopped at the apartment of a friend who was a doctor and also a Flynn-fan. It is not clear whether Errol's condition or the doctor's interest prompted the visit – perhaps both. In any case, Errol was injected with a pain-killing drug.

He seemed to revive. In fact, he was so chipper that he for a while entertained his friends with some of his own special brand of stories and clever imitations of such stars as Bette Davis and John Barrymore.

At last, he grew tired and said he needed to rest. When the doctor offered him a bedroom, Errol, because of his painful back, lay not on the bed but on the floor. To both the doctor and Beverly, he insisted that he was beginning to feel much better.

Earlier, when he had had hepatitis, a Swiss doctor had warned him about his liver and told him that he was going to die soon. But Errol recovered, he made his last pictures, and he wrote *My Wicked, Wicked Ways,* which ended with the words: "The second half-century looms up, but I don't feel the night coming on."

Darkness fell soon afterwards, because on the floor of that doctor's bedroom in Vancouver, Errol drifted into a sleep that turned into death. Many news sources reported that Errol collapsed in the street or died in an ambulance on the way to hospital – or both. It is probably true, though, that he made a stylish exit, announcing mock-heroically as he entered the doctor's bedroom, "I shall return."

He had taken a long time to wear out – an amazingly long time for one who had lived as he had. The coroner said that the body was that of an old man, and though the official cause of death was a heart attack, the autopsy revealed evidence of other illnesses, some of long standing – malaria, hepatitis, gonorrhea and tuberculosis among them.

The Films of Errol Flynn gives a thorough and absorbing inventory of the 'collapses' that punctuated his career. Their recital here will show that the perfect specimen had been a sick man for years, not merely technically but with intermittent attacks of serious illness.

While *Captain Blood* was being filmed, Errol collapsed on the set with malaria. In September 1941, while *They Died With Their Boots On* was in production, he collapsed in the elevator of a medical building. No detailed or convincing explanation was given. In 1942, the star collapsed from 'fatigue' on the set of *Gentleman Jim.* But this was a few weeks after his rejection by the army and navy, and 'fatigue' was a mild coronary. In May 1943, he again collapsed on a set, this time during the making of *Northern Pursuit,* the illness being tuberculosis.

So much for the man who 'dodged' World War II and was made to suffer by the press for doing all his wartime heroics on the screen.

Errol was buried at Forest Lawn Cemetery on 20th October 1959. During a dignified service, the eulogy was delivered by Jack Warner, whom Errol had sworn to outlive, perhaps only half in jest. The pallbearers were Mike Romanoff, Guinn ('Big Boy') Williams, Jack Oakie and Raoul Walsh.

10

Never Say Goodbye

To say that Errol Flynn committed suicide would be foolish, but some men keep strange rendezvous with destiny, and he had done little to avoid his premature death.

In 1952, another star, John Garfield, had died early, as if in answer to some perverse inner need. The victim of witch-hunting in the McCarthy era, Garfield found himself black-listed and almost unable to work in films. Perhaps in obscure defiance, he lived up to and beyond his physical limits, ignoring a collapse on the tennis-court that should have warned him of impending – but possibly avoidable – death. He was a mere thirty-nine.

Though he lived longer, Errol's end was not so dissimilar.

He knew the risks. The auguries had been clear. But he chose to pursue a destiny that he could probably not have put into words. His death was not sheer carelessness but had, rather, a tragic inevitability; and to say that he did not "feel the night coming on" was more literary bravado than an expression of truth.

There is an appalling sense of waste about such prematurely spent lives. The star of *Robin Hood* and *The Sea Hawk* had surely accomplished enough. But he could, the late films show, have done more.

If he ever committed one, dying early was his only real crime.

There is a saying: the sword wears out the sheath; and whatever *daimon* drove Errol Flynn, his life and death illustrate the maxim perfectly. He had his own ideas about the nature of his compulsion: "Not drink, not drugs, not sex. It is curiosity. This has got me into all my troubles, successes, failures. I cannot resist looking into a garbage can or a good book, a new or an old bottle, a bar, an empty or a full paper bag. I cannot resist anything that holds out an antenna towards me, or looks alive or dead, or scarlet or putrid or beautiful. I am drawn towards light, towards darkness, towards brilliance, stupidity, monstrosity."

Jack Warner called him "one of the most charming and tragic men I have known", and Bette Davis described him as "handsome, arrogant and utterly enchanting".

Errol was of course many men. He was both clown and courtier. He was a man of action and something of a seer. He was a good but not a great actor. He could be charming to women and brutal as well. He was a boor and a braggart. Even though he published books, he was an author *manqué*. He was an athlete and a sick man – occasionally both at the same time.

It is significant that among his films one of those he loved best was *The Cruise of the Zaca* – that "thoughtful little picture". He said that his greatest fear was "the fear of mediocrity", but he was rarely mediocre. He was a compulsive chaser, but in a sense sex was or became a burden to him. He found women made better friends than men. "In my early days," he wrote, "I was brought up to hear it said that you can never have a real woman friend, that male friendship is deeper, like Damon and Pythias. That is not true – not in my book . . . I learned, when the cards were down, who were my friends and who were not – and these [two women] were . . . When the going is tough, give me a woman for a friend. If they happen to care for you, they will go farther than any man."

It might be said that Errol Flynn died like the great king in Seneca's tag:

> Notus nimis omnibus
> Ignotus sibi.
>
> (Too known to all the world,
> To his own self all unknown.)

But that would be unfair both to Errol, who knew much of himself with uncanny perception, and to those among his friends and admirers who saw beneath the surface of the swashbuckler and the rogue.

Towards the end of *My Wicked, Wicked Ways,* he remarks, "In me, contradiction itself, as a principle, finds its own *raison d'être.* I am convinced of the validity of contradiction. There are many worlds. Each is true, at its time, in its own fashion."

But he had always found it hard to sustain such a mood of philosophical solemnity, and often others saw only his frivolity.

Scott Fitzgerald, whose life-story in many ways prefigured Flynn's, met him in 1937. His career in trouble and his personal life all but destroyed, Fitzgerald might well have been immune to the Flynn charm, especially as the moviestar was rising while he, Fitzgerald, was battling debt, alcoholism and failure as a writer. Three years before, he had published *Tender Is The Night,* and though the author was not to know it, if one big composite picture had been created of all the roles Errol was to act in his string of adventure-films, the result would have been a character with striking similarities, at least psychologically, to Dick Diver in his own novel. This screen composite would have matched the Dick Diver of the early part of the book, with his eagerness to please, his good manners, his courtesy of the heart; while the Dick of the later chapters could have served in some ways as a picture of Errol the man, particularly as he neared fifty. (Nor, for us, need the parallelism end there, for writer and actor had much in common – including, strangely enough, the fact that they were both beaten up by the police, an indelible experience that Flynn described in his autobiography and that Fitzgerald incorporated into *Tender Is The Night.)*

But Fitzgerald, with a short time to live, was never to make or be in a position to make such a comparison. His encounter with the star was brief, but he wrote, "He seemed very nice though rather silly and fatuous."

Nearly ten years later, Sterling Hayden saw a different Flynn.

If superficially like Errol, – a moviestar, a sailor, a rebel and an adventurer – Hayden was essentially a different sort of man. Nevertheless, the two had even more in common than Flynn and Fitzgerald and were passing through similar psychological crises. Hayden's terse comments in the pages of *Wanderer* say much about the man who had been blurred by the actor: "We talked of ships. He knew places and people – but not ships... A certain wistfulness was evident in the empty set of his face, and I gathered, since he offered no counter-talk, that his war had been passed at Warner's . . . He listened well, drinking remorselessly, but with no apparent effect."

This judgement of Errol as a sailor should not, let it be noted, be set aside lightly. Hayden ran away to sea when he was seventeen and was captain of his own brigantine at twenty-two.

Some, though they knew him well, never got close to what lay beneath the sometimes "silly and fatuous" exterior. There is Ann Sheridan's much quoted comment: "He was one of the wild characters of the world, but he had a strange, quiet side. He camouflaged himself completely. In all the years I knew him, I never really knew what lay underneath, and I doubt if many people did."

Errol realized well enough the gap in his life between the myth and the man.

In the film *The Tall Men,* Robert Ryan says of Clark Gable, who is playing a Flynn-type soldier of fortune and impeccably virile hero, "There goes the only man I ever respected. He's what every boy wants to be when he grows up and what every man, looking back, wishes he had been."

For years, Errol played that character, and he found the repetition increasingly frustrating and exhausting, the more so because what he depicted on film was so different from the person he saw shaving every morning. Errol the man was not the romantic hero; he was at once more real and less whole. As the years went by, he would tell himself, "You are an impostor, Flynn. In real life you don't do any of the things you do on the screen. You are no more capable of that kind of action in real life than a choirboy."

And yet he had a kind of bravery, even if it was not of the obvious physical type, but rather the quiet fortitude of the man who suffered failure and the ordeal by trial for rape. Jack Warner put it this way: "His gallantry was of the spirit, not just motion picture scripts. His courage was as staunch as his manner was gay."

If Errol's 'private' life was lurid, the compulsive impetus had much to do with his series of heroic screen-roles. He had to be bad because up there – on the screen – he was so good.

Edmund Wilson once described James M. Cain as the "*âme damnée*" of Hollywood, pouring into his stories all the things that Catholic censorship prevented him from depicting in his screenplays. Something similar could be said of Errol, whose noble film-self was the antithetical twin of the Flynn who proved so rich a source of material for the gossip-columnists.

In a mood of singular melancholy, he wrote, "I generally deny that I was ever a good actor, but I know I have turned in a half-dozen good performances . . . I portray myself as wicked, hoping I will not be regarded as wicked."

An interesting riposte came years afterwards from Lewis Milestone, who directed him in *Edge of Darkness:* "Flynn kept underrating himself. If you wanted to embarrass him, all you had to do was tell him how great he was in a scene he'd just finished playing; he'd blush like a young girl and, muttering 'I'm no actor', would go away somewhere and sit down.

"Maybe not enough people knew Flynn well. I not only admired him as an actor, I liked him very much as a person. I knew him as a perfect host, a marvellous connoisseur of good food and wine. His faults harmed no one but himself."

Such – apparent and real – were the contradictions of Errol Flynn.

As he himself made clear, "There are many worlds. Each is true, at its time, in its own fashion."

He had a knack, and that probably harmed him more than anything else. The man who looked a better dancer and fencer than he really was, was not a sham, because his grace and panache were real. But his tragedy lay in the difference between how good he was and how good he looked. He was, perhaps most of all, one who did everything too easily and few things well enough.

Actors and entertainers decline in popularity for many reasons, sometimes because, like Judy Garland, they seem to be working at destroying the reputation built up over many years.

Errol Flynn never did that, though some of his later pictures might have seemed like documents of his own disintegration. Those resistant to his qualities as a star asserted that his popularity waned in the early 'fifties because he was too bland, because audiences wanted, to use the words of Scott Fitzgerald, heroes "with more corrugated surfaces". As a criticism, that makes poor sense, if only because by that time, Errol had acquired the unmistakable signs of erosion and experience. However, despite the attention aroused by the posthumous publication of *My Wicked, Wicked Ways,* there was probably a slump in public interest in the star for a year or two after his death.

Now we can see that there is even more definitely a revival in Errol's popularity. There is a storybook irony in the way that television, which helped to mar or destroy the careers of so many filmstars of the 'thirties and 'forties, has also bestowed upon them second careers, later fame and, for some of them, resurrection after literal death. Film-festivals have played their part, too.

The great stars never die, it seems: they do not even fade away. They merely strut and parade on a smaller screen, and there, on television all over the world, Errol is still his unique and dashing self – the handsomest rascal ever to come riding down the pike.

When I was a boy, his presence on film could fill a cinema with warmth, could inspire an audience as perhaps only the great performances can. His more heroic exploits would set the cheers ringing among the juvenile cinemagoers to whom he was what every boy wanted to be when he grew up.

Nobody can be certain that Errol Flynn has attained immortality – an unsure and overrated commodity at best. But it is likely that he will continue to warm our hearts and stir our blood for many years to come

Bibliography

Aadland, Florence, as told to Lisa Janssen. *The Beautiful Pervert.* New York: Novel Books Inc., 1965.

Aadland, Florence, as told to Tedd Thomey. *The Big Love.* New York: Lancer Books, 1961.

Cutts, John. 'Requiem For A Swashbuckler' in *Cinema*, Vol. 3, no. 5. Beverly Hills, California: Spectator International Inc., 1967.

Eddington, Nora, as told to Cy Rice. *Errol and Me.* New York: Signet Books, 1960.

Flynn, Errol. *Beam Ends.* London: Cassell and Company Limited, 1937.

Flynn, Errol. *Showdown.* London: W. Foulsham and Company Limited, 1952.

Flynn, Errol. *My Wicked, Wicked Ways.* New York: G. P. Putnam's Sons, 1959; London: William Heinemann Limited, 1961.

Fowler, Gene. *Good Night, Sweet Prince: The Life and Times of John Barrymore.* New York: Viking Press, 1944; London: Hammond Hammond, 1949.

Higham, Charles; and Greenberg, Joel. *The Celluloid Muse: Hollywood Directors Speak.* London: Angus and Robertson, 1969; New York: New American Library, 1972.

Kael, Pauline. *Kiss Kiss Bang Bang.* Boston: Little, Brown, 1968; London: Calder and Boyars, 1970.

Moore, John Hammond. *The Young Errol.* Sydney: Angus and Robertson, 1975.

Morris, George. *Errol Flynn: A Pyramid Illustrated History of the Movies.* New York: Pyramid Publications, 1975.

Niven, David. *The Moon's a Balloon.* London: Hamish Hamilton Limited, 1971; New York: G. P. Putnam's Sons, 1972.

Niven, David. *Bring on the Empty Horses.* London: Hamish Hamilton, 1975; New York: G. P. Putnam's Sons, 1976.

Roeburt, John. *Get Me Giesler.* New York: Belmont Books, 1962.

Schickel, Richard. *The Stars.* New York: The Dial Press, 1962.

Thomas, Bob. *King Cohn.* New York: G. P. Putnam's Sons, 1967; London: Barrie and Rockliff, 1967.

Thomas, Tony. *Cads and Cavaliers: The Gentlemen Adventurers of the Movies.* New York: A. S. Barnes and Co. Inc., 1973; London: Thomas Yoseloff Limited, 1973.

Thomas, Tony; Behlmer, Rudy; and McCarty, Clifford. *The Films of Errol Flynn.* New York: Citadel Press, 1969.

Thomey, Tedd. *The Loves of Errol Flynn.* Derby, Connecticut: Monarch Books Inc., 1962.

Walsh, Raoul. *Each Man In His Time.* New York: Farrar, Strauss and Giroux, 1974.

A Flynn Filmography

1 *In the Wake of The Bounty* (Expeditionary Films, 1933)
Directed by Charles Chauvel. With Mayne Lynton, John Warwick, Patricia Penman.

2 *Murder At Monte Carlo* (Warner Brothers First National, 1934)
Directed by Ralph Ince. With Paul Graetz, Eve Gray.

3 *The Case of the Curious Bride* (Warner Brothers First National, 1935)
Directed by Michael Curtiz. With Warren William, Donald Woods, Margaret Lindsay.

4 *Don't Bet On Blondes* (Warner Brothers, 1935)
Directed by Robert Florey. With Warren William, Guy Kibbee, Claire Dodd.

5 *Captain Blood* (Warner Brothers First National, 1935)
Directed by Michael Curtiz. With Olivia de Havilland, Lionel Atwill, Guy Kibbee, Henry Stephenson.

6 *The Charge of the Light Brigade* (Warner Brothers, 1936)
Directed by Michael Curtiz. With Olivia de Havilland, Patric Knowles, David Niven, Henry Stephenson, Donald Crisp, Nigel Bruce.

7 *Green Light* (Warner Brothers First National, 1937)
Directed by Frank Borzage. With Anita Louise, Margaret Lindsay, Cedric Hardwicke, Walter Abel.

8 *The Prince and the Pauper* (Warner Brothers First National, 1937)
Directed by William Keighley. With Claude Rains, Billy and Bobby Mauch, Alan Hale, Henry Stephenson.

9 *Another Dawn* (Warner Brothers, 1937)
Directed by William Dieterle. With Kay Francis, Ian Hunter.

10 *The Perfect Specimen* (Warner Brothers First National, 1937)
Directed by Michael Curtiz. With Joan Blondell, Edward Everett Horton.

11 *The Adventures of Robin Hood* (Warner Brothers First National, 1938)
Directed by Michael Curtiz and William Keighley. With Olivia de Havilland, Basil Rathbone, Claude Rains, Patric Knowles, Alan Hale.

12 *Four's A Crowd* (Warner Brothers, 1938)
Directed by Michael Curtiz. With Olivia de Havilland, Rosalind Russell, Patric Knowles.

13 *The Sisters* (Warner Brothers, 1938)
Directed by Anatole Litvak. With Bette Davis, Anita Louise, Ian Hunter.

14 *The Dawn Patrol* (Warner Brothers, 1938)
Directed by Edmund Goulding. With Basil Rathbone, David Niven, Donald Crisp.

15 *Dodge City* (Warner Brothers, 1939)
Directed by Michael Curtiz. With Olivia de Havilland, Bruce Cabot, Ann Sheridan.

16 *The Private Lives of Elizabeth and Essex* (Warner Brothers First National, 1939)
Directed by Michael Curtiz. With Bette Davis, Olivia de Havilland.

17 *Virginia City* (Warner Brothers First National, 1940)
Directed by Michael Curtiz. With Miriam Hopkins, Randolph Scott.

18 *The Sea Hawk* (Warner Brothers First National, 1940)
Directed by Michael Curtiz. With Brenda Marshall, Claude Rains, Flora Robson, Alan Hale, Henry Daniell.

19 *Santa Fe Trail* (Warner Brothers First National, 1940)
Directed by Michael Curtiz. With Olivia de Havilland, Raymond Massey, Ronald Reagan, Alan Hale.

20 *Footsteps In The Dark* (Warner Brothers First National, 1941)
Directed by Lloyd Bacon. With Brenda Marshall, Ralph Bellamy, Alan Hale.

21 *Dive Bomber* (Warner Brothers First National, 1941)

Directed by Michael Curtiz. With Alexis Smith, Ralph Bellamy, Fred MacMurray.

22 *They Died With Their Boots On* (Warner Brothers First National, 1942)
Directed by Raoul Walsh. With Olivia de Havilland, Arthur Kennedy, Gene Lockhart.

23 *Desperate Journey* (Warner Brothers First National, 1942)
Directed by Raoul Walsh. With Ronald Reagan, Nancy Coleman, Alan Hale.

24 *Gentleman Jim* (Warner Brothers First National, 1942)
Directed by Raoul Walsh. With Alexis Smith, Jack Carson, Alan Hale.

25 *Edge of Darkness* (Warner Brothers First National, 1943)
Directed by Lewis Milestone. With Ann Sheridan, Walter Huston, Nancy Coleman, Judith Anderson.

26 *Thank Your Lucky Stars* (Warner Brothers First National, 1943)
Directed by David Butler. With Olivia de Havilland, Ann Sheridan.

27 *Northern Pursuit* (Warner Brothers First National, 1943)
Directed by Raoul Walsh. With Julie Bishop, Gene Lockhart.

28 *Uncertain Glory* (Warner Brnthers First National, 1944)
Directed by Raoul Walsh. With Paul Lukas, Jean Sullivan.

29 *Objective, Burma!* (Warner Brothers First National, 1945)
Directed by Raoul Walsh. With William Prince, George Tobias.

30 *San Antonio* (Warner Brothers First National, 1945)
Directed by David Butler. With Alexis Smith, Paul Kelly, Victor Francen.

31 *Never Say Goodbye* (Warner Brothers First National, 1946)
Directed by James V. Kern. With Eleanor Parker, Patti Brady.

32 *Cry Wolf* (Warner Brothers First National, 1947)
Directed by Peter Godfrey. With Barbara Stanwyck, Richard Basehart.

33 *Escape Me Never* (Warner Brothers First National, 1947)

Directed by Peter Godfrey. With Ida Lupino, Eleanor Parker, Gig Young.

34 *Silver River* (Warner Brothers First National, 1948)
Directed by Raoul Walsh. With Ann Sheridan, Bruce Bennett.

35 *The Adventures of Don Juan* (Warner Brothers First National, 1949)
Directed by Vincent Sherman. With Viveca Lindfors, Robert Douglas.

36 *It's A Great Feeling* (Warner Brothers First National, 1949)
Directed by David Butler. With Doris Day, Jack Carson, Dennis Morgan.

37 *That Forsyte Woman* (Metro-Goldwyn-Mayer, 1949)
Directed by Compton Bennett. With Greer Garson, Walter Pidgeon.

38 *Montana* (Warner Brothers First National, 1950)
Directed by Ray Enright. With Alexis Smith, Douglas Kennedy.

39 *Rocky Mountain* (Warner Brothers First National, 1950)
Directed by William Keighley. With Patrice Wymore, Scott Forbes.

40 *Kim* (Metro-Goldwyn-Mayer, 1951)
Directed by Victor Saville. With Dean Stockwell, Robert Douglas, Paul Lukas.

41 *Hello, God* (William Marshall, 1951)
Directed by William Marshall. With Sherry Jackson.

42 *The Adventures of Captain Fabian* (Republic, 1951)
Directed by William Marshall. With Micheline Presle, Vincent Price.

43 *Mara Maru* (Warner Brothers First National, 1952)
Directed by Gordon Douglas. With Ruth Roman, Raymond Burr.

44 *Against All Flags* (Universal, 1952)
Directed by George Sherman. With Maureen O'Hara, Anthony Quinn.

45 *The Master of Ballantrae* (Warner Brothers, 1953)
Directed by William Keighley. With Anthony Steel, Roger Livesey.

46 *Crossed Swords (Il Maestro Di Don Giovanni)* (United Artists, 1954)
Directed by Milton Krims. With Gina Lollobrigida, Cesare Danova.

47 *Lilacs In The Spring (Let's Make Up)* (Everest Pictures, 1955)
Directed by Herbert Wilcox. With Anna Neagle, David Farrar.

48 *The Dark Avenger (The Warriors)* (Allied Artists, 1955)
Directed by Henry Levin. With Joanne Dru, Peter Finch.

49 *King's Rhapsody* (Everest Pictures, 1955)
Directed by Herbert Wilcox. With Patrice Wymore, Anna Neagle.

50 *Istanbul* (Universal, 1956)
Directed by Joseph Pevney. With Cornell Borchers, John Bentley.

51 *The Big Boodle* (United Artists, 1957)
Directed by Richard Wilson. With Rossana Rory, Gia Scala.

52 *The Sun Also Rises* (Fox, 1957)
Directed by Henry King. With Tyrone Power, Ava Gardner, Eddie Albert.

53 *Too Much, Too Soon* (Warner Brothers, 1958)
Directed by Art Napoleon. With Dorothy Malone, Efrem Zimbalist.

54 *The Roots of Heaven* (Fox, 1958)
Directed by John Huston. With Trevor Howard, Eddie Albert, Paul Lukas.

55 *Cuban Rebel Girls* (Exploit Films, 1959)
Directed by Barry Mahon. With Beverly Aadland.

Errol Flynn himself directed and appeared in the short film *The Cruise of the Zaca.* He also appeared in another short, *Deep Sea Fishing,* and played the lead in the unfinished *William Tell,* which was being directed by Jack Cardiff

A Flynn Discography

There is a wealth of recorded music from the Flynn pictures, though not all of it is available in current catalogues. Of the following albums, though none is without interest, the best are the magnificent RCA Classic Film Scores series. In a special category, the album issued by Delos Records contains rare recorded interview-material, principally with Errol Flynn himself.

RCA SER 5664 (LSC 3330) *The Sea Hawk: The Classic Film Scores of Erich Wolfgang Korngold.*
Superbly recreated by the National Philharmonic Orchestra of London, conducted by Charles Gerhardt, and produced by George Korngold (the composer's son); the first of the RCA series; contains music from *The Sea Hawk, Robin Hood, Captain Blood* and *Escape Me Never*; plus music from the scores of other Warner Brothers productions.

RCA ARL 1-0185 *Elizabeth and Essex: The Classic Film Scores of Erich Wolfgang Korngold.*
Music from *The Private Lives of Elizabeth and Essex, Another Dawn* and *The Prince and the Pauper;* plus music from the scores of other Warner Brothers productions; National Phil., Gerhardt, etc.

RCA ARL 1-0912 *Captain Blood: Classic Film Scores for Errol Flynn.*
The films are *The Sea Hawk, Captain Blood, Robin Hood* (Korngold) (previously unrecorded selections); *The Adventures of Don Juan, They Died With Their Boots On, Dodge City* (Max Steiner); *Objective, Burma!* (Franz Waxman); *The Sun Also Rises* (Hugo Friedhofer); National Phil., Gerhardt, etc.

RCA SER 5695 (ARL 1-0136) *Now, Voyager: The Classic Film Scores of Max Steiner.*
Contains one track devoted to *The Charge of the Light Brigade;* National Phil., Gerhardt, etc.

RCA ARL 1-0422 *Casablanca: Classic Film Scores for Humphrey Bogart.*
Contains one track devoted to *Virginia City* (Max Steiner), the only Flynn picture in which Bogart ever appeared; National Phil., Gerhardt, etc.

RCA ARL 1-0813 *Classic Film Scores for Bette Davis.*
Contains the theme for Elizabeth from *The Private Lives of Elizabeth and Essex;* National Phil., Charles Gerhardt, etc.

WARNER BROS. 1438 *Music by Erich Wolfgang Korngold,* conducted by Lionel Newman.
Recorded August, 1961; a rare collector's-item; the tracks include music from *The Private Lives of Elizabeth and Essex, The Sea Hawk, The Prince and the Pauper* and *Robin Hood.*

DELOS F25409 *Requiem for a Cavalier:* a sound picture of Errol Flynn/*The Adventures of Robin Hood:* symphonic suite by Erich Wolfgang Korngold conducted by the composer.
Requiem for a Cavalier is an abridged version of a 1968 radio documentary by Tony Thomas for the Canadian Broadcasting Company. As well as soundtrack excerpts from *Captain Blood, They Died With Their Boots On, The Sun Also Rises* and *Robin Hood,* the album contains the recorded voices of Nora Eddington, David Niven, Vincent Sherman and Flynn himself. An indispensable item for the Flynn admirer.

The *Robin Hood* suite is a transcription from four 78's (never issued commercially) made in 1938. There are ten score-segments and a narration by Basil Rathbone. Despite the dated sound, the suite, with Korngold conducting, is uniquely fascinating.

RCA LSB 4105 *Violin Concerto* in D, op. 35 by Erich Wolfgang Korngold/Jascha Heifetz and the Los Angeles Philharmonic Orchestra conducted by Alfred Wallenstein.

EMI EMD 5515 *Violin Concerto* in D, op. 35 by Erich Wolfgang Korngold/Ulf Hoelscher and the South German Radio Symphony Orchestra conducted by Willy Mattes.

In the concert-hall and on records, Errol Flynn lives on in one of Korngold's most appealing and brilliant works, for the first movement of the violin concerto opens with a melody from *Another Dawn* and the finale, variations in rondo-form, is based on a theme from *The Prince and the Pauper*.

RCA 2311 *The Sea Hawk/Of Human Bondage* by Erich Wolfgang Korngold – The National Philharmonic Orchestra of London conducted by Charles Gerhardt.

A curiosity – a 45-single, presumably issued as a trailer for the Classic Film Scores series; *The Sea Hawk* segment is an edited version of track one from RCA SER 5664 (LSC 3330)

Index

L

M

N

O

U

V

W

Z